Sober, I am not Afraid

An autobiography by
Martin 'Jim' McFadden

Published by Martin McFadden

Copyright © Martin McFadden 2008

ISBN Number 978-0-9559403-0-9

Edited by Strawberry Media 2008, Co. Donegal, Ireland

Dedicated to

Daddy and Mammy –
James and Sadie McFadden

In memory of my father who died on 20th March 1993
In memory of my mother who died on 8th October 1998
May You Rest in Peace

I thank God for both of you. You were always there for me especially when I needed you most. Despite my challenging character and wild ways you loved me just as I was, and gave me the support I needed during the dark times. You are my inspiration and I will always love you.

Acknowledgements

When I decided to undertake my personal journey and to give an honest account of my life, especially through the darker years, I had much support from my family and friends.

To my loving wife Liz who is, and has been, my rock for the past 14 years. Thank you for your understanding and unconditional love.

To my sisters Mary Teresa and Bridie and my brother Eunan and his wife Nancy, and all my nephews and nieces, and in memory of Joseph – thank you all for your patience, kindness and love during my wild times! Without your support I don't think I'd be here today.

To my late brother Edmund, a great big brother, who was always there for me, day and night.

To all my mates with whom I had the craic, thanks for all the laughs, during the highs and lows.

Finally, thanks to Joanne Sweeney, my editor, who helped make this book a reality – bringing it from my hand-written words on a page to a credible book for sale in the shops.

> *"I didn't have a camera,*
> *So photos they were few,*
> *But whatever I can remember,*
> *I would like to share with you."*

The stories told in this book are true and correct. However, the names of the characters have been changed to protect their identity.

Prologue

Where It All Began

'They took it from the Jims,' my father would say. My mother, meanwhile, would reply by saying, 'We all know who the Jims are and where they came from, but nobody seems to know who or where your family came from.' That was an exchange of conversation my parents had on several occasions after the Guards called to our house looking for us for whatever reason. When I was growing up I was quite often involved in some sort of a prank or mischief, or what we used to refer to as, 'just out acting'. But as I got older and started drinking I found myself fighting regularly and smashing up various pubs.

Eight years ago I started doing my family tree as I knew there was always a bit of mystery surrounding my father's side of the family. My mother's family tree meanwhile seemed straight forward. My father's parents had both been married before with children. For reasons unknown however, these children seemed to disappear and weren't part of the second family.

My father and his brother Eddie had two half brothers and one half sister that they never met. My father often talked about them and wondered whatever came of them. I have now finally solved our family puzzle.

My Uncle Dennis was reared with family relatives and died tragically in Philadelphia in 1961. His body was recovered from a river. He was a single man with no children. My other uncle, Patrick Joseph, and my aunt Mary Agnes, were both admitted to Nazareth House in Derry under the recommendation of Canon James McFadden, who was their granduncle. The Canon was a powerful figure during that time and much has been written about his life since.

Mary Agnes was killed in Hackney, London in 1924. She died after falling from a moving bus. Mary was buried in a pauper's grave in Leytonstone in London. I recently located her grave and placed a cross on it. Mary was single and didn't have any children. Patrick Joseph moved to America and married his wife Harriet, with whom he had two daughters, Irene and Patricia. They lived in

California where Patrick owned his own store. In September 1941 they were involved in a car accident while travelling on holidays. Their car got hit by a train. Harriet died that day. Patrick died the following January as a result of his injuries. Irene and Patricia both survived. They were aged five and nine at the time of the accident.

I only recently made contact with my cousin Patricia for the first time. Sadly Irene died in 1995 before I got the opportunity to meet her.

Despite the extent of the tragedy and sadness in my family, my research has finally proved to be worthwhile and very rewarding. We now have a big family reunion planned. It was during my research into my family tree that I decided to write this book. A wise man once told me that 'bad writing is better than a good memory', and that reminds me of another saying, 'A good bed and a good pair of shoes are very important because when you're not in one, you're most likely to be in the other.'

Chapter One

The Beginning of the Madness

I was born in 1963 in the house which is still my home today. My father, James McFadden, was from Cashel, Creeslough and my mother, Sadie McLaughlin, was from Dunmore, Carrigart. I was the youngest of five siblings. I had two brothers and two sisters. Edmund was the eldest, next came Mary Teresa, then Eunan and Bridie. I was always referred to as the baby or 'the wane' (short for wee one). I'm not sure how old I was when my mother took me to a holy well known locally as Doon Well. For some reason my hair still hadn't started to grow so my mother bathed my head in the well. Stories have been told of people who were cured from various illnesses after attending the well. After our visit my hair started growing. I do remember however, being in fourth class when I got ringworm in my hair. I missed most of that term as a result and had to re-sit fourth class the following year. However, I can still boast about my good head of hair forty years on.

We didn't play much football on our breaks. Instead we played marbles, hounds and hares, and rounders. Most of the time we would just wrestle with each other but it usually got out of hand. At that time it was acceptable for teachers to slap their pupils and from my own memory they abused the system. I'm surprised today that none of them have been summoned to appear in front of a tribunal of some sort with a case to answer.

In my final year at national school I was admitted to hospital to have my appendix removed. It was Christmas Eve. I remember the nurse asking me if I believed in Santa, to which I replied, 'yes'. I knew by giving that answer I would get a present. I had my operation that night and when I awoke the following day, Santa had delivered. I got a colouring book and crayons. I really appreciated it even though I knew the score on Santa. I always loved Christmas as a child. We were always so excited on Christmas Eve, eagerly awaiting the visit of our friend. We really treasured the presents he brought us. It's just so different now for children as there is much more money around, so I'm grateful for my memories which were so special and had that magical feeling.

I never finished my final year at national school and didn't sit the exams. That was the end of my education. I was thirteen years old. I never went to secondary school. I remember saying to my father, 'It's only prigs that come out of there.' That same year I started my first job as a kitchen porter in our local hotel. The pay was £15 per week. I worked split shifts six days a week. The hours were 8am to 3pm and 5pm to 10pm. The work was hard. Most of the staff were crazy and the craic was good so I fitted in quite well.

I remember one time myself and the fellow working alongside me having a falling out with one of the cooks. We found out that when he sent his pots down to the pot wash for us to scrub they would be slightly burned, thus making it harder for us to clean them. A few days later, when we realised it wasn't just an accident, we decided on an easy way out of it. So instead of taking time to wash the pots we started dumping them in the rubbish bins. It wasn't long until there was a scarcity of pots and a big inquiry into what was happening to them. As there were a large number of people employed, and quite a few around my own age, we were always up to some sort of mischief. The management were busy trying to keep us under control. Sometimes they would have no option but to sack the dossers. I saw quite a few of my work colleagues 'walk the line' before it eventually came to my own turn some seasons later.

We spent our breaks just messing about down in the village. We would often borrow a football from one of the shopping baskets and have a kick about on the street. During the summer it was usually quite busy, and I'm sure we annoyed a lot of people. One day however, our new pastime came to a sudden end when one of us kicked the ball into the local chemist and smashed some expensive pottery in the process. One other day myself and another fellow lifted our mate and placed him inside a shopping trolley and let him loose down the main street at the mercy of oncoming traffic. The trolley came to a halt after it crashed into a wall and thank God our mate escaped uninjured.

That reminds me of a similar incident. My Uncle had been confined to a wheelchair after he suffered a stroke. Myself and my cousin, both aged about 13, took him out and were taking it in turns to push the chair. We had just reached the top of a hill and were breathless. Our Uncle was a bit of a character and was slagging us about being unfit. We then let go of the wheelchair with the good intentions of catching it again before anything happened. However, it gathered speed so fast that it careered down the hill and we couldn't catch it. Our Uncle was screaming and praying out aloud. We could only watch on helplessly as the chair hit the ditch throwing our Uncle headfirst into the hedge. Thank God he didn't suffer any serious injuries from that incident.

During my first season working in the hotel I bought myself a bicycle to transport me around. It was second hand and cost me one week's wages. I also bought a large wall clock for our home. It was new and also cost £15. That clock is still in good working condition and hangs in my hallway to this day.

My memories of my childhood years are simple and happy ones. Prayer played a big part in our home and we recited the Rosary each day. Our door was always open, so if a neighbour or visitor came in they would usually kneel down and join in. We always went to Mass on a Sunday but myself and my mates got into the habit of standing at the back of the Church discussing the week's events. Quite often we were told to shut up by another Mass-goer but that only made us worse and so we would just talk louder and make more noise.

The hotel season ended in September so it would remain closed until the following Easter. All of my mates had now started secondary school and I had a lot of time on my hands. When we met up we would spend most of our time just walking or quite often getting chased along the roads as we were usually up to some form of mischief. We could be walking and running for miles, sometimes through dark fields and falling into ditches and drains.

One night I remember we borrowed a large white sheet from somebody's clothes line. We walked down to our local graveyard and took up position. We were taking it in turns, and when we would see a car approaching one of us would stand in the middle of the road. We had the sheet draped over our bodies, with both hands outstretched moving up and down. We were having great fun at that until finally the Gardaí arrived in an unmarked car and gave chase. We all ran off through the fields in different directions. I remember approaching a dead end with a thick hawthorn hedge in front of me. I could hear the garda saying, 'We have you now.' I then covered my face with my hands and dived right into it and hoped for the best. I ripped my clothes in the process as I crashed through it but did manage to make my escape unharmed.

We enjoyed the chase so much that we used to go robbing apples from orchards just hoping for a chase. Bonfire night was a big occasion for us and we gathered tyres for weeks in advance. Farmers' silage pits were always a good place to steal them from. I'm sure if we had asked for them in the first place, we would have probably been given them, as quite often when we took them we would trample a field of hay in the process. Looking back now it was hard work but it was all part of the entertainment.

Myself and my mate came up with a plan one day. We sort of made the shape of a man out of timber. We then got some old clothes and dressed him. We used a head of a cabbage for a head, and once it got dark we took it in turns to carry him down to the main road. We then placed him lying on the roadside with his head in next to the ditch with the rest of his body sticking out onto the road. We lay behind the ditch waiting for our first car to come along but we didn't have long to wait. It was hilarious to watch as the driver had to swerve to avoid hitting our buddy. You can imagine his surprise and shock when he went to see who was lying there. We lifted our buddy and ran up the field and out of sight, but once the coast was clear we set him out again. However, the next car didn't see our buddy in time and drove over his legs. By the time the car screeched to a halt we had picked up our badly injured buddy and once again disappeared out of sight. What made this particular incident so funny was the fact that all the occupants of the car were French, so we couldn't understand a word they were saying, as they franticly searched for their victim. Later during the night we had to run and abandon our buddy, but sometime later when we knew we were safe my mate turned to me and said, ' Jesus I have lost my Daddy's fucking wellingtons.'

Thank God I never started smoking. I remember my father watching me one day when I was drinking a bottle of mineral. I would have been 13 or 14. At the time, whatever way I attacked the bottle he noticed something unusual and said to me, "if you ever start drinking you will become an alcoholic." How true that would later turn out to be.

My first memory of taking alcohol was when I was about 14. It must have been a special occasion in our house as there were a large group of people gathered. As the party was in full swing I sneaked a drink outside and drank it. I don't know how much or what it was but I do remember falling and being unable to get up again. The power had gone from my wee legs. There were five concrete steps leading up to our front door and I had to crawl on my hands and knees to get back inside again.

The following Easter I started back working in the hotel. This time I got promoted to front hall porter. I was now wearing black shoes, black trousers, a white shirt and black dickey bow. It was almost impossible to keep your shirt clean for a full day. You were always watching over your shoulder as it was possible to get hit by anything ranging from a dirty brillo pad or dish cloth to a dirty bucket of water. Sometimes you might have the fire hose turned on and then find yourself running for cover. I suppose I gave as good as I got. One day a waitress just broke a raw egg over my head and what a mess it made. It was several days later before I got my chance for revenge. As she was waiting to be served at the hot plate I sneaked up behind her and grabbed an egg and attempted to smash it over her head. What I didn't realise was that the egg had been hard boiled so as well as almost knocking her out, I almost broke my hand in the process.

We also used to lift other members of staff and place them on top of the open wheelie bins before running off. One day a member of staff, who was a bit on the slim side, got his bum stuck in the open bin. Other staff members had a struggle trying to release him as we had already disappeared. Although we spent a lot of time messing about, the job itself could get very busy and sometimes you were under so much pressure. You sometimes felt like running away from it all when it did get busy.

My hours were now 8am to 7pm six days per week. As well as carrying the visitor's luggage you also had to serve tea and sandwiches. I remember that wet days were sure to be busier than dry days as most of the guests would be sitting about and feeling sorry for themselves. You never knew when a bus tour might stop off for afternoon tea. When that happened it was just crazy and nothing short of slave labour. One day I was already run off my feet, when I noticed three coach loads stopping outside. They were American tourists. I met them at the front door and informed them that we didn't serve afternoon tea and so I recommended a nice little café down the street. They had turned to get back on board their buses when the manageress appeared out of nowhere. She approached the bus load of tourists and after discovering what had happened she said, 'Of course we are still serving afternoon tea, so come on in and Martin will take your orders'. I would just like to add that I didn't receive any tips for that service.

That season I got a pay rise of £3 per week. It was my second season and I was now on £18 per week. Another day I was in the dining room preparing sandwiches and a female member of staff grabbed me by my privates. She had caught me unawares and made me jump. My hand was holding the bread knife at the time and I accidentally hit her and cut her hand. I felt terrible as she required seven stitches to that same wound. Under the circumstances of how that incident happened it was all kept very hush hush and not many people knew the true story.

I did join the local athletic club for a period and ran in a few races but I was never going to be a Sebastian Coe so I soon gave up on that. I also had a go at football but was equally as useless at that. I didn't possess the necessary skills that were required for the game and usually when another player would pass me out with the ball I would try and trip him up and bring him to the ground one way or another. The rare few times I got selected to play I would've got sent off again by the referee.

Some nights myself and a few mates would go and play bingo. It was more for the craic than anything else. We would be that busy chatting and messing we would end up missing numbers and possible winnings. I noticed that during the last game of the night a large number of players would start making their way towards the exit door. There was always a large queue for the fish and chip van outside and I guessed that's why they wanted a quick exit. So, once someone would call 'check' on that last game, they would drop their bingo books and make a dash for the door. One night I called 'check' just for a laugh and as expected the books got thrown away as there was a stampede for the door. I then sat tight for a while until they finally realised it was a false alarm.

It was hilarious as they were scrambling under tables and chairs looking for, and arguing about, their bingo books.

Another pastime I enjoyed back then was card playing. There were raffles in different houses and the prizes would vary from a donkey, goose, to maybe two hens. One winter's evening, we found ourselves playing for a goat. But whoever was lucky, or maybe unlucky enough to win it, would just put it up for raffle again the following week. Nobody had collected or looked to see about their prize in months and when one winner finally went to claim his prize, we discovered that a local character had killed it and eaten it - after he himself had won it at one of the earlier raffles. It later transpired that my brother actually helped him to butcher it. We had been playing for a long time for a prize that no longer existed.

Other forms of entertainment we found at the local youth club. It was held every Saturday night in the parish hall. Myself and my mates didn't seem to have any interest other than messing about and acting the eejit. I remember one night I got up onto the stage. There was a large pair of curtains which I grabbed hold of in Tarzan style. I walked back and still holding the outstretched curtains I raced out and swung over the open floor. As I was swinging back in again I could hear the sound of the curtains tearing. I landed on my arse on the stage floor, underneath the now unattached, and damaged, curtains. When I was confronted about it I said I just imagined I was Tarzan. The committee eventually barred myself and a few mates as we were always messing about. Most of the other lads our own age would have been trying to court the local girls but we would have just referred to them as sissys or mama's boys. Later, after a meeting one night, the committee decided enough was enough and that was the end of our Saturday night youth club. When the priest asked us what we wanted instead, I replied, 'A boxing club!'

Chapter Two

Buying My First Motorbike – A Honda 70cc

My third season started with another pay increase of £3. I was now earning £22 per week as a front hall porter. Although I hadn't started drinking yet (I never did smoke), I now had become addicted to slot machines. I remember on a few occasions losing all my wages on pay day. That was a horrible experience. But myself and a few mates had now discovered a method of fiddling the machines. First of all, we learned that if you flicked a two pence coin hard enough in the slot it would register as a ten pence. Secondly, we discovered that the back panel on the machine could be wedged open enough for us to get our hand inside and hold the reels. For a short period of time we were hitting the jackpot every day. Some of the time our winnings would amount to very little as we would just get the two pence coins back again. When we complained about this to the shop owner we were told that if we hadn't put them in in the first place then it wouldn't be happening. Thank God I got away from that habit and never did get into any other forms of gambling.

Some of our mates had now got cars and we soon started playing a very dangerous dare. Two of us at a time would sit on the roof top. We would sit side by side, holding on to each other with one hand, while placing our other hand in the open window. We would hold on for sheer life as the driver raced up the road. It was a miracle none of us ever suffered any serious injuries or lost our lives as a result of that stunt.

But we did figure out a less dangerous form of entertainment – hiding in the boot of the car. One of us would sometimes put ourselves inside the car boot to the horror of the passengers we would pick up along the way. The routine was that after the driver had picked up a passenger, the fellow in the boot would start banging and screaming for help. We found this hilarious and whoever was driving would then turn the music up loud, as if to drown out the cries for help. Whoever was brave enough to go in the boot made sure it was left slightly open because once you were locked inside you were left there at your mates' mercy. We also discovered it was a great way of gaining free admission to football matches, sports days or stock car racing.

That same season I bought my first motorbike. It was a Honda 70cc. My father gave me the money to pay for it. It cost £300. I was supposed to repay my father on a weekly basis. It was a good job I hadn't borrowed the money from a bank as my name would have been black listed. Some weeks I gave my father money and some weeks I didn't, but my father never once mentioned it. My parents never took any money from us towards our keep but I'm sure there were times when they were struggling.

I was all business now with my new motorbike and for the first two weeks I took great care and was very careful on the road. However, as time went on I just became more daring and reckless. One day, myself and a mate who had a Honda 125cc were touring about. We both had passengers on. I was struggling all day trying to follow and keep up with him. That evening we were driving down a very steep part of road with a bridge and very sharp corner at the bottom of it. My mate had more experience and also more sense, so as he starts to slow down I say to myself, 'Now this is my fucking chance to pass them and show them how it's done.' I never eased off on my throttle and as I zoomed past I even gave a big wave of my hand so as to show off. My passenger was now gripping me harder and harder and needless to say I never managed to take the corner. We ended up crashing through the hedge. Luckily we missed the stone bridge. We didn't receive any bad injuries from the fall and, although the bike was a bit damaged, we got it repaired.

That was my first accident on my bike but it wasn't going to be my last. I was so reckless and fearless back then that it got to the stage that anyone who knew me would not sit on with me. I crashed several times with passengers on. When I knew they were becoming frightened it just made me even more daring and reckless. One night I had two mates on. One was sitting behind and the other fellow was sitting on the handlebars. I was going full throttle down a hill and suffered a blow-out on my front wheel. Needless to say the three of us got an unexpected tumble.

One other day I was driving home from work and saw a girl I knew walking along the road. I stopped and offered her a lift but she said there was no way she was getting on with me! I promised her I would drive easy and after swearing on at least a dozen saints' names she agreed. She was wearing a skirt and when she had just about got her leg lifted over the seat, I took off. I didn't give her enough time to place her feet on the foot stands. So, as I'm now racing over the road, I have one female passenger holding onto me for dear life and screaming her head off. It was only when we reached her house that I realised what had really happened. Her bare leg had been touching the bike's hot exhaust pipe. She suffered minor burns to her leg, which I was genuinely sorry about.

Chapter 3

Getting Sacked from the Hotel

The following Easter I started into my fourth season as a hotel porter. It was also going to be my last as my term of contract was going to be terminated abruptly. My wages had now increased by the usual amount. I was now earning £25 per week. My heart was not in the job anymore. I was approaching my 18th birthday and would soon be able then to sign on at our local social welfare office and claim unemployment benefit. I knew that amounted to £18 per week so I figured it would be pointless working like a slave for £7 extra per week. I also knew I could get plenty of work on the bog with my brother which would leave me much better off financially.

After my birthday, which was in May, I informed the manager that I was quitting. When he asked me why, I told him the truth. He then threatened to call the Social Welfare office to say that I had a job, meaning that I wouldn't qualify for unemployment benefit. I wasn't sure if he would carry out his threat so I accepted his offer of a pay rise of £5 per week and returned to work. I knew at that particular time they were under pressure for staff but I had made my mind up and was determined on leaving, one way or another. I then figured out that all I had to do was to get myself sacked and I knew that wouldn't be a problem. As well as not doing my own work I set about disrupting everybody else's and just creating mayhem and causing havoc about the place. A few days later I got my wish and my walking papers. He was so annoyed with me that day, I was sure he was going to thump me one. My memories of working there are both good and bad.

After I got sacked that day, I got on my wee Honda 70 and arrived up on the bog, where I knew my father and brother would be working, trying to save our turf. After I told them what had happened, my father told me not to worry about it as there would be plenty more opportunities. That is one thing I will always be grateful for. I had the most understanding and loving parents in the world. They were always there for us when we needed them. I always thank God for having them for so long, especially when we needed them most.

That summer I got a lot of work on the bog. I also managed to buy myself a bigger and more powerful motorbike. It was a Honda 250cc. I bought it in Derry for £180 sterling. I now had much more power, but I still hadn't learned any lessons from my previous accidents. One day I met a mate coming from Sunday Mass. He was cycling on his racing bike. He had a few steep hills to go up on his way home so I suggested I would give him a tow. He was a bit reluctant at first but I assured him I would drive easy. I managed to get my hands on a length of rope and attached it underneath the handlebars of his bicycle, connecting it to the rear suspension of my motorbike. I started off slow but kept increasing my speed along the way. I remember looking over my shoulder a few times and seeing my mate holding on for all he was worth, trying to keep himself and his bike on the road. He admitted that if I hadn't stopped when I did he was just going to let go, as his hands and arms were so tired and weak. It was a miracle that day that we survived that crazy stunt without injury or worse.

You see, I would just get this buzz inside me at times and very often I would have put myself and others at risk. One other day I was out for a spin on my motorbike and was driving past a golf course. I was alone and on the spur of the moment I just drove onto the course and up through the links. There was a large group of golfers enjoying a leisurely round of golf. But when they spotted me some of them began running trying to get out of my way. Others, who seemed to be a bit braver (and angrier), started swinging their golf sticks at me, trying to knock my head off. As I was racing out the small exit gate trying to make my escape, I remember closing my eyes for a few seconds; sure I was going to get struck with a club. As usual I wasn't wearing a helmet.

One other day I was down in a local village, which was also a seaside resort. There was an amusement arcade which had two rows of gaming machines lined back to back up the middle of the floor. The place was packed and every machine was occupied. I figured if nobody walked out in front of me I would have enough room to do a quick circle of the hall on my motorbike. After I got the doorway clear I raced in but wasn't prepared for what happened next. As I slowed down at the top of the hall to take the corner two very angry old women attacked me. One was battering me with her umbrella, while the other was thumping me with her handbag. The whole place was now cheering as I struggled to drive out through the mayhem. One other night myself and a mate drove into a local nightclub on his motorbike. We drove in one door and up through a packed dance floor before making our exit out the fire doors. This time I was the passenger.

There was a track nearby, at the Sandy Hills (local nickname for the sand dunes), where motorbike scrambling races were held. Several times I would have gone in on my 'road bike' to see if I could complete a stage. For the record, I always practiced when it was empty. However, as my bike wasn't built for rough ground I was usually sent flying over the handlebars.

Chapter 4

Carrigart Boxing Club

Carrigart Boxing Club was formed in 1980. There was a barn next to the priest's parochial house which was converted into a gym. It was a two storey building. Upstairs was used for training on the punch bags while downstairs had a boxing ring for us to spar in. Training was three nights per week, Monday, Wednesday and Friday. It was a great pastime for the young men of the parish, as we now had something to keep us out of trouble. Our trainer had made it clear he would not tolerate or have any messers in his club. We also went running a few nights a week so when our first tournament was held in the parish hall, we were fairly fit. We were both excited and nervous as everyone wanted to impress in front of family and friends at their first big fight. It was a big occasion for all concerned, including our trainers and committee members.

On the evening of the fight, I was in the changing room preparing myself. I noticed a boxer from one of the visiting clubs going through his warm up routine. He had the look and the moves of someone who seemed to know what he was doing, and I remember thinking to myself that I wouldn't like to be the fellow who was fighting him. When it was my turn to box, I climbed into the ring. I was nervous and praying to myself for divine inspiration. Then I heard the compere calling out our names. I knew my opponent was not the fellow I had been supposed to fight and I nearly shit my pants when I saw the boxer I had been eyeing up earlier, now climbing into the ring opposite me. I turned to my trainer and said, 'That's not the fellow I am matched with,' to which he replied, 'Never mind who he is, just go out and box him!' I did go out and try my best but I was well and truly beat and out-boxed in every round. Most of the other boxers from our club won their fights that night so it was a credit to them and our trainer. They did Carrigart Boxing Club proud that night on its first ever tournament. We all continued training and when our second tournament was due we were well prepared and ready for action. During my second fight I got hit with a combination of hard punches in the first minute of the first round and ended up knocked out with my arse on the canvass. My boxing career had got off to a very bad start.

One other night, we travelled to a tournament in Kincasslagh in West Donegal. Myself and a mate, who hadn't been matched to fight, decided to climb in through a toilet window rather than pay at the door. After a struggle we got squeezed through but then realised we were in the ladies toilets. Luckily enough there were no ladies present, powdering their noses or whatever, so we just put our heads down and walked into a packed hall. Shortly after that my trainer approached me and informed me I had just been matched to fight. I then had to go out to my bus for my gear. I told the men who were on the door collecting the money that I must have lost my ticket. I remember my fight that night was tough going. At the end of the second round I told my trainer that I was seeing six eyes. He said to me, 'Well, I suppose you had better aim and try and hit the two in the middle.'

After the club closed for the season I never did go back, so that was the end of my boxing career. I suppose my boxing record was now pretty similar to my education and employment history to date - not very impressive to say the least.

The following year, I got a job with Donegal County Council. It was only on a Back to Work Scheme, and although it was only a temporary position it was good while it lasted. We were employed at our local pier, building a slipway to enable them launch small boats and jet skis. The basic pay was £98 per week but, as we had to work according to the tides, it meant there was plenty of overtime and weekend work. There were large wire baskets called Gabriels that we had to fill with stones, tie them closed and attach them to the next one to form a wall to keep the tide at bay.

I was still driving my Honda 250cc and one morning, travelling to work, I had yet another lucky escape. The road was covered with snow and ice and as I was driving down a hill I skidded and fell off my bike. The bike came to a halt when it hit the ditch, but I now found myself sliding down the road towards an oncoming car. The driver managed to get stopped just in time. It was a lady driver and she was speechless as she watched me getting back onto my bike. I then gave her a big wave as I continued on my way. I later sold that bike and bought myself another 250cc motorbike. This time I went for a Suzuki. But I still hadn't got used to the idea of paying for tax or insurance. One night, I was driving through my local village and a Garda on duty signalled for me to stop. I thought I would take a chance so I just kept on going as fast as I could and made my escape. Shortly afterwards my luck finally ran out when I got stopped at another checkpoint. Later, at court, I was fined a total of £56 for not wearing a helmet, for having no drivers licence and no tax or insurance.

Chapter 5

Drinking

After the work on the slipway was completed, my Back to Work Scheme came to an end. I now found myself unemployed again. Although I missed the money, I wasn't too bothered or concerned about going out of my way to look for work. Unlike most of my mates, who were either working, or doing FAS courses, I was just happy to doss about. I never was career minded or anyway ambitious. During the summer months, myself and my brother got plenty of work on the bog, cutting and saving the turf for different clients. Our wages started off at £15 a day which later increased to £20 per day. As I was also in receipt of unemployment benefit I was happy enough with my casual employment. Other times I would get the odd day's work gathering potatoes.

I had now also started drinking and from my very first drink it was obvious that I was going to have a problem with it. If I had the money, I would just keep drinking until I was out of my head or sometimes just fall asleep. During my early years of drinking I would have got into a lot of trouble in the pubs and the nightclub scene. I can't really blame alcohol for all of it, as I was a bit on the wild side back then and got a great buzz from it. Many times, after I came off second best and received a good thumping, I would say to myself 'Fuck, this craic is no good. I must stop this oul' carry on.' But after a few days, when I would start to recover again, I would then change my mind and go out looking for a rematch or revenge. I saw myself going out at weekends and fighting Friday, Saturday and Sunday nights. I had no sense, or fear of danger during that time. I then also found myself barred from most bars and clubs in my own and surrounding areas, and so it meant I often had to travel out of town. Quite often I could end up alone in a bar on the other side of the county.

It still didn't matter where I was or what my chances were. As the old saying goes 'I would rise a row in an empty house.' During that time, I figured if I didn't go out on Friday or Saturday nights I would have all my money for a good session on the Sunday and would go to the pub after Mass. Me and my mates were always looking for ways and methods of getting drunk cheap and quick. We used to try drinking out of straws and also just drinking as fast as we could swallow it. We used to also buy poitín at £3 per bottle. Other times we would buy the kit and make our own brew of beer. Usually it would just taste horrible, but we didn't care as it was only the effect we wanted.

I remember one time I was on a wild binge of poitín and home brew. My brother arrived to give me a lift to our local Garda Station, where it was compulsory to sign on a weekly basis for your dole or unemployment benefit. When he looked at me and saw the shape I was in, he asked, 'Do you know what day of the week it is?' I replied, 'Yes, it must be Tuesday, but what month is it?'

After returning from a nightclub one night I brought my mate in for a drink of poitín. I had decided to make punch out of it. So, after boiling the kettle, I produced my bottle and continued to make what I assumed to be two good strong drinks. It was sometime later that I discovered that I had been serving us both Doon Well holy water!

I remember one day I was gathering potatoes for a local farmer and found a bottle of poitín in the field. I didn't know or care how old it was and after drinking it I climbed out over the fence and went in search of more drink. That night I ended up in a nightclub, still wearing my work clothes. I also got into another one of my battles and received a wound on my arm which required ten stitches. Another time, I remember a group of us fighting outside another nightclub! I went there knowing there was going to be trouble. I had been drinking all day and had consumed a large amount of alcohol. During the scuffle, I went crashing through a large glass window. I was only wearing a t-shirt and received another large cut to my arm which required 36 stitches – 18 stitches internally and 18 externally. Myself and two of my mates were then arrested and put into the same patrol car.

On our way to the hospital, I remember grabbing the Garda hat and placing it on my own head. Once inside the hospital, I hopped into a wheelchair and raced down a corridor almost knocking the Garda over in the process. He was so disgusted with me that he remarked, 'That fucker is not near right in the head, racing about there and the arm hanging from him.' He then left us there and after I got stitched up I had to make my own way home.

My next decent bit of employment was at a house known locally as Claggan House. It had also been the house where my Grandmother was born, and before that it was home to my Great Great Grand Uncle Canon James McFadden, who was involved in the famous evictions in Gweedore.

Money was no problem now for the new owners of this property and there was a large body of men employed to carry out the renovations. Tradesmen were earning £40 per day and myself and other labourers were earning £25 per day. It was the summer of 1986 and it was considered good money at the time. I remember one day myself and my mate were trying to see which one of us could wheel the most blocks in our wheelbarrows. We both had so much weight on, that the tyre on both our barrows seemed flat. On seeing this, our boss and employer then ordered two new wheelbarrows no questions asked. Hence, there was no shortage of money.

Chapter 6

My Accident

At weekends we used a local bus service that would take us to and from a nightclub in a town about 20 miles away. There were live bands playing and it was always busy, so it was the place to be for the craic. As usual, I was there on a Saturday night and one night met a girl who was home on holidays from Glasgow. We hit it off from the beginning and arranged a date for the following night, in the same venue. I didn't go drinking during the day on the Sunday as I was really excited and looking forward to my date. At about nine o'clock I went down to my local bar where I got the bus. The bus was always packed and sometimes you had more craic travelling on it than in the actual nightclub. That night I met my date and we had a really nice time. I travelled home with her on her bus. She was returning home to Glasgow in the morning. We exchanged phone numbers and promised we would see each other again. I then set off walking for home which was about seven miles away.

It was after 4am. It was still fairly dark and I was wearing dark clothes. I also had a large amount to drink. I ran for short distances and when I got tired I would resume walking. The last thing I remember is approaching a part of the road that had a bad corner and a sort of a dip in the road. My next memory is waking up and my family by my bedside.

I was in the Intensive Care Unit in Letterkenny General Hospital. I was told I had been involved in a serious car accident. I had suffered horrific injuries to my body. Both my legs were shattered. My knees and ankles were badly broken and my shoulder, hip, pelvis and groin were also injured.

While I was waiting to be transferred to a Dublin hospital, my brother-in-law Daniel Cannon, who had been a patient in the medical ward of Letterkenny General Hospital, died. His remains left the hospital at the same time as I was being airlifted to Dublin. It must have been a difficult time for our family. It was about six weeks later before I heard of Daniel's death. I had been too ill to receive such sad news. That was 25th August 1986. I was 23 years old. I do remember travelling in the helicopter. I was drifting in and out of consciousness. I was then admitted to the ICU ward of Dr. Stevens' Hospital. My chances of survival remained at 50-50 for the first two weeks. When I did start to show signs of recovery, I was told I might have to have my leg amputated, as my legs and ankles had suffered such serious injury. I was also told I might not walk again. At times I remember being in so much pain and suffering that I cried out aloud for mercy. My recovery was going to be a slow and painful experience.

One morning I had a near death experience. I remember going into a deep sleep and imagining I was drifting down a long dark tunnel. My injuries required extensive surgery. I had plates and wires inserted to both my knees and ankles. I also had to have extensive skin grafting to large parts of my body, mainly my groin area and both my legs. I was confined to bed for quite some time and was fully dependent on the excellent care and attention of the nurses and doctors. When I was well enough to leave I.C.U., I was transferred to a large 18-bedded ward. It wouldn't have been easy for my family visiting me on such a regular basis, but they were always by my side. From our home to Dr. Stevens' Hospital was a good five hour drive each way, so it must have been very difficult for them to arrange transport. Sometimes they would travel by car and sometimes travel down by bus. My friends and neighbours also visited me on a regular basis. I received so many get well cards and Mass cards. It was the love and support of my family and friends and their constant prayers that gave me the courage and strength to want to survive.

I remember the day I was told of Daniel's death. I broke down crying and a nurse who was comforting me told me I now had enough to worry about in terms of ensuring my own recovery. She then suggested we both say a prayer to Daniel and ask him for his help, which we did. I then asked her if she could take me to a phone as I wanted to ring my sister. Both my legs were fitted with plaster, one full cast and one below my knee. The kind nurse then got me into a wheelchair. She placed a large board underneath my bum and leg to support the weight of my full cast. The payphone on my floor was out of order so the nurse then brought me down in the lift to the floor below. Although I still couldn't walk, it was a great feeling to get a break from my ward and into new surroundings. The nurse then said she would leave me to talk in private and would come back for me in ten minutes. I had finished my call before the nurse arrived back so I decided I would try and make my own way back to my ward. I managed to wheel myself over to the lift. I figured that if I reversed my chair into the lift I would be able to drive straight out at my own floor. I got into the lift without a problem but once the doors closed I realised I was in bother.

My leg with the full cast was now protruding about two feet out from my seat, which prevented me from getting in close enough to press the lift buttons. I found myself stuck inside a lift that was stationary. I'm not sure how long I was there for, but it seemed like ages. After a lot of effort, I managed to slide out of the chair enough to reach the button but by the time I was back seated the door had closed again. I tried that same stunt, with exactly the same results, on three more occasions before my nurse in shining armour came to my rescue.

I remember the thirst I had was unreal. One day it was so bad that I chewed the drip that was going into my vein. When I did start to recover and was allowed to drink mineral, I always wanted to make sure I had a good supply beside my bed. I suppose it was part of my addiction and related to my alcoholism. One day I asked the lady who was going around the wards with her mobile shop for a few bottles of mineral. She had nine bottles in her shop. She then counted thirteen that I had stored in my locker and underneath my bed.

My lady friend also visited, which helped to lift my spirits. We were also exchanging love letters which gave me something to look forward to. A friend had brought me in a walkman which gave me endless pleasure, listening to my favourite music. Even today, when I hear the songs of that time, it reminds me of my stay in Dr. Stevens' Hospital. The nurses were so kind and understanding. They would sit by my bedside, hold my hand and talk to me when I would be feeling down or sorry for myself.

The driver of the car also visited me on a regular basis which was nice. I reassured him to not feel one bit guilty or bad about our accident as it was in no way his fault. When he drove around that corner that morning I was already laying on the road. Apparently I had been the victim of a hit and run sometime prior to that.

I was now three months in hospital. My wounds were healed but my skin grafting was so tender to touch. I had the plaster casts removed from my legs but walking was proving to be a very difficult task indeed. When the physiotherapists stood me on my feet, I would feel so weak that I would have to sit down immediately before I would collapse. I felt just like a baby having to learn how to walk all over again. I remember once laying awake in my bed. It was about four in the morning. I got a very strong feeling that I could walk again. There was another patient also awake in the bed next to mine. He had the power of his legs so I asked him to get me a walking frame. It was then I took my first steps. It was an unbelievable experience and I knew from that moment that I was on the road to recovery and could walk again. I did, however, get reprimanded by the night nurse for getting out of bed unattended.

A few days after that I was taken to theatre. As my left knee had been completely shattered, with most of my knee cap missing, I could not bend my leg. In theatre they froze it and tried to force some movement or flexibility. After applying pressure but without any success they had to stop, otherwise it would have just broken. My doctor then told me there was not much more they could do for me, so I could start making arrangements for going home to Donegal. I was told I would never regain full movement of my right ankle and that my left leg would remain permanently straight. The first thought I had then was that I wouldn't be able to kneel at Mass.

I was now so excited and looking forward to going home. There was a bus service to and from Letterkenny General Hospital to various Dublin hospitals, which I could get later that same day. I didn't have any clothes, as they had to be cut off me when I was first admitted to hospital on the morning of my accident. I got on the bus that evening outside Dr. Stevens' Hospital. All I was wearing was a pair of pyjamas and a dressing gown. My bedroom slippers had been cut to make room for my two badly swollen feet. It was the end of November. The frost was thick on the ground and I was really cold. My family had offered to come down by car and lift me but I reckoned I would be ok on the bus. I suppose it was my rough and ready attitude, but I suppose I was also thinking of saving them the hassle.

When we stopped at Monaghan at a café on our way home, I couldn't very well go in so the kind bus driver brought me out a cup of warm tea and a sandwich. I really enjoyed and appreciated it. My family met me at Letterkenny Hospital with a new outfit. During my three month stay in hospital I had lost almost three stone in weight. It was a great feeling that night, getting dressed in my new clothes and going home with my family. Our Parish Priest visited me the following day and said, 'Martin, you know you can't be carrying on the same way as before your accident'.

Although I had made a miraculous recovery, I still had a long way to go. I was still dependent on the aid of two crutches and was told I would require extensive physiotherapy three times weekly for an indefinite period of time.

Chapter 7

Getting Engaged

My first appointment at the physio department of Letterkenny General Hospital got off to a very bad start. I found the exercises painful and difficult. I got talking to another patient who was also a bit of a character so we decided to go for a drink. The physiotherapists had shown us our exercises and had left us alone to do them. Both of us were on crutches. So we just walked out while the therapists were working with other patients. We didn't even bother making another appointment. We then walked, or should I say, hobbled down the street and into a bar. We both got very drunk. I never saw that gentleman after that day and often wondered how he got on. I also forgot his name. That was my first and also my last time to attend physio.

That night I got a taxi home. The driver stopped outside our gate. As I was walking up towards our gate I forgot about the cattle grid that had been fitted in my absence, so my left crutch went straight down in between the bars. As I was trying to balance myself I stuck the second crutch between two more bars. So, left without any support, I then fell flat on my face onto the ground. I had to crawl up the driveway but eventually did make it up to our door.

After being involved in such a serious accident and now getting a second chance at life, I still hadn't learned my lesson or copped myself on. The following day I went drinking again and got myself arrested. I went into bars I had been barred from before my accident, and in all fairness to the Landlords, they shook my hand and said I was welcome. They probably assumed that I had settled. I was wild before my accident and maybe I was now just trying to prove a point to myself, because that day I got myself barred again in every pub I went into. I also got arrested for criminal damage and assault, as I started swinging my crutch about when I got refused more drink. There was a female neighbour in our house the night the Gardaí brought me home. When she heard what I had just done, she turned to my mother and said, 'Sadie, I know what must have happened to him. When he lost all his blood in the accident it was replaced with a madman's.'

Myself and my lady friend remained in regular contact by phone and letters. I now made arrangements to go to Glasgow so that we could spend Christmas and New Year together. I could get a bus in Carrigart which would take me to Glasgow for £46 return. The ticket would remain valid for three months. It was a big occasion for me as it would be my first time out of my own country. I was also looking forward to seeing my old friend again. We had a really nice Christmas. On New Year's Eve we got invited to a house party that lasted all night long. I remember we left it the following morning. We were walking down a street and passed a church while Mass was going on. I hadn't a clue what time of day or night it was and thought we were outside a packed nightclub. I wanted more drink so I said to my friend, 'Let's go in here for one.' She then informed me it was Mass that was being said and not a band playing. I then went off on my own against my friend's wishes.

That same day I ended up fighting outside a bar in Glasgow. Later, when I got on a bus to get me back to my friends house, I realised I hadn't kept any money for the fare. I then had to get off the bus again and find someone who would be kind enough to give me the required amount. I was lucky and met a lady who gave me £2. I never was interested in football and didn't realise Celtic and Rangers had been playing earlier that same day, so here I was staggering around some street in Glasgow wearing a big green jumper.

I returned home to Carrigart shortly after that. I had to attend Dr. Stevens' Hospital as an outpatient on a regular basis. My lady friend then came over for another holiday. We really did enjoy each other's company so much and missed each other when we were apart. So we decided we would get engaged with a view to getting married.

For the next few months I just spent my time between Glasgow and Carrigart. I was receiving Disability Benefit. I was expecting to receive compensation from my accident sometime in the future so looking for a job never crossed my mind. I had no interest whatsoever in doing a FAS course or re-sitting my exams, which were of course sensible options. But at that stage in my life I was far from being sensible and seemed happy to just doss about without facing up to reality.

My brother Edmund was also living in Glasgow at this time, so I used to look forward to meeting up with him as it would always result in a good oul' session. One day we were both in the horrors. We were craving for a drink and we didn't have any money. We went into a Social Security office and I approached the lady on the counter and told her a big sad story. I explained that I had arrived in Glasgow three days previously with no money and no place to stay. I then said I had been sleeping in an old car and hadn't eaten in ages. She had sympathy on me and directed me to another office where I would receive Counter Payment. She told us what bus to get, but as we didn't have the fare we started off walking.

That same day Edmund and myself somehow ended up walking onto the middle of a motorway, holding on to the crash barrier to keep us from falling out in front of the traffic. I can't remember how on earth we got onto it but we had to walk for ages to reach an exit. I still wouldn't have been that steady on my feet and I remember every time a large truck would pass, we would have to hold tight and hope for the best. We did eventually manage to get off it. Later, at traffic lights, I was making an attempt to cross the street, Edmund shouted for me to wait, but I replied that it was ok as 'the wee green man was on.' Edmund replied, 'Don't rely on that wee fucker as he might let us down.'

We did eventually reach our destination and I received a payment of £29. I thought I was rich, as when you're skint and desperate £29 is a lot of money. We then went into a nearby pub for a well deserved drink. I was ordering double whiskeys so fast Edmund said to me, 'Remember, it was only £29 you received and not £290, you wee fucking head case.'

Chapter 8

Getting Unengaged

As I got my bus at the Gorbals for my return journey home, I remembered that I didn't have any money. I was hungry on the boat but I knew I would be ok once I got home. I had to attend Dr. Stevens' Hospital for another check-up. But I was now walking without the aid of crutches. Despite not being able to bend my knee, I was becoming stronger and was much faster on my feet. It was surprising as I wasn't receiving any physio, and in fact I was still behaving recklessly and getting myself into dangerous situations. My fiancée knew I had a serious drink problem and had asked and advised me to address it. She also warned me that if I didn't settle down she was going to call our engagement off. At that stage in my life I didn't realise I was an alcoholic so I continued on drinking and getting myself into more trouble.

One night, after yet another fight, I ended up damaging my knee. I had to go back into Dr. Stevens' Hospital for another operation as the pins and wires that had been holding my leg together were now protruding out through my skin graft. As I waited to be taken to theatre I was told that my operation was cancelled as an emergency had cropped up. I had now made friends with a girl from Co. Galway whose operation was also cancelled. The exact same thing happened both of us on two more occasions. On the fourth day, we still were waiting and fasting. It was 4.45pm and we were both starving with the hunger. We assumed our operations were going to be cancelled once again, so my lady friend fetched a large cake somebody had brought her. After I had devoured my half, the porter from theatre arrived to take me for my operation. I was now in a bit of a predicament. I didn't want to have to cancel again so I said I was still fasting. I remember coming out of my operation, I imagined my head was stuck to the table and I couldn't move it. For the short space of time it lasted I remember being frightened. I don't know if it was the side effects of having eaten the cake, or if anybody else ever had a similar experience.

After my operation I was transferred to a three-bedded ward. One of the patients in the ward with me had crashed his motorbike, while the other was a big man who had come second in a fight. Both were confined to bed. The biker now had a good supply of beer by his bedside, which were presents from his biker friends. So we were rich with cans of Smithwicks. On the second night after my operation, he asked me would I like to have a drink with him. I gladly accepted. I was acting the role of barman and asked if I should give our boxing friend a drink. My mate replied, 'No way. That big fucker might get out of bed and half kill the two of us.' We both got drunk that night in our ward. I remember a nice young nurse saying to me, 'It's up to yourself what you do with your life. If you want to destroy it then that's your own choice.'

When I was getting discharged, my doctor told me I would most certainly develop arthritis in both my legs, but mainly in my knees. I was also advised to go back for physiotherapy on a regular basis. Needless to say, I never did and continued on drinking and living life on the edge.

After getting myself into another row, I now found myself appearing at our local court with a case to answer. I received a one month suspended prison sentence for assault and causing criminal damage to a public house. I was also ordered to keep the peace and observe good behaviour for a period of three years. Looking back, the only people I was hurting were my family. My parents must have been worried sick about me.

My lady friend had now carried out her threat and ended our relationship. She said she could not put up with my drinking or wild living any longer. She wished me luck in the future and said she genuinely hoped everything would work out for me in the end. My solicitor also wrote me a sharp letter stating that he was not very impressed with my behaviour. He also advised me to settle down and keep on the right side of the law. He warned that another court appearance would result in me being sent to prison which would, in turn, seriously damage and affect my claim for compensation. I was now really missing my lady friend's company and, as I was more than likely to get myself into more trouble at home, I decided I would go to London and try and make a new life for myself.

I now had an appointment coming up in Dublin with doctors from the Insurance Board. I made arrangements to get the boat later that same night for my onward journey to London. While I was waiting for my bus in Letterkenny to take me to Dublin, a member of the travelling community approached me and asked for some money. I offered him whatever loose change I had in my pocket. He didn't seem very grateful and said, 'Can you not do any better than that?' I knew now I had made a mistake in becoming involved with him. I didn't want to give him any paper money and I knew from his manner that he wasn't just going to forget about it and walk away. He was also much bigger than me and as he became more aggressive, I told him to calm down and I would see what money I had in my pocket. I now had butterflies in my stomach, as I knew I had to box him one. So once again I took my chances and hit him a right hook, hoping to catch him unawares, and get myself out of town in one piece. I didn't fancy going into my medical check-up in Dublin with two black eyes or worse.

I did manage to make it to Dublin in time for my appointment. I was so relieved when my check-up was over. I was now feeling both excited and nervous, thinking about my move to the big smoke.

Chapter 9

Going to London – My First Day at Work

I had over four hours to wait until I got my bus out to Dun Laoghaire, where I would get the boat to Holyhead and then get another coach down to Victoria Coach Station in London. It was an overnight sailing and we were due to arrive in London about 7am the following morning. Whatever Punts I had on me, I decided I wouldn't be needing again for a while, so I started on a pub crawl. As I made my way towards Gardiner Street and Busaras, with four or five pints in me, I started knocking back double brandies. I can remember being very drunk on the boat but I don't remember either getting on or getting off it. The next morning, I remember waking up on the coach down to London and being seated next to a nun. God knows what bullshit I was talking while I was awake, as she gave me a nice pair of beads and said she would pray for me.

We arrived at Victoria Coach Station on time and I phoned my mate Frank who lived in Acton. He told me I could stay there until I got myself sorted. Frank then sent his friend down to meet me. It was still early morning when I landed at my new digs and after being shown my room I planned on checking out the tubes and getting a bit familiar with the area. Another one of the lodgers, whom I also knew soon appeared and after giving me a big bear hug and welcoming me to London, he suggested we go for a drink. It sounded like a good idea at the time and, needless to say, it ended up in another all day session.

The next morning Frank woke me at 6am and gave me a lift down to Shepherds Bush. There was a contractors' office there where I could look for a job. I knew one of the managers personally and he told me that if I was ever in London and wanted a job, to give him a shout. After receiving a good welcome at the office, I was then sent with a foreman called Mick out to a job near Liverpool Street Tube Station.

For some reason Mick wasn't driving, so we both travelled by tube out to the job. As I was only a labourer, Mick put me to work sweeping and just tidying up around the yard. At lunchtime Mick asked if I wanted to go for a pint and I accepted. After four pints we returned to the job with both of us in good form. It felt great to be back working again and I was looking forward to my whole new life in London. It was nearing the end of the shift and Mick asked if I was interested in some overtime, which I also accepted. Then, shortly after 7pm, Mick said we would go for another pint and that he would put me in for four hours overtime. We headed back to the same bar we had been in earlier and after consuming another four pints, we made our way to the tube station. Mick suggested I should stay at his place that night and we could travel together in the morning out to the job. It sounded like a good idea at the time.

Mick was living near Shepherds Bush. Once we sat down on the tube, Mick fell asleep, so at every stop I had to shake him to ask him where we were. When we finally arrived at Shepherds Bush tube station Mick said we would go for one more pint before we went home. Well, as usual, one lead to two, and two to three and so on. So a number of pints later Mick turned nasty towards me. Mick was born and bred in London and we were drinking in his local. It seemed to me that with him being my boss and me just off the boat, he probably thought I'd listen and take it. Well, I couldn't take any more and when I told him that I thought he was full of shite, he asked me if I knew where I was and who I was talking to. When I replied that, 'I didn't give a fuck,' he apologised. So after one more we made our way home.

While we were staggering back to his house, he explained that his wife was black and that she would probably rear up on us in the beginning, but for me to keep quiet and just ignore her, as she would eventually calm down. Well, true enough, once we entered the house we were met by one very angry woman. But once she was finished shouting her head off at Mick, she then turned her anger at me. I thought to myself, 'Jesus, my first day isn't going so well now'. As usual, my wild streak took over and so I told them to stick their house where the sun didn't shine and that they were both welcome to each other. Maybe I said something else to upset them because Mick's wife said that if I didn't leave immediately she was going to call the police. I soon made a very speedy exit and the next thing I knew I was walking down a strange street in London, drunk and not knowing how far I was from my digs.

After walking for what seemed like ages, I flagged down a taxi and gave him my address. I can't remember how much it cost but when I finally did make it back to my digs, my roommate Noel was getting up for his work. It was only then that I realised the time. So I turned and made my way down to East Acton tube station. I was feeling the worse for wear from the lack of sleep and the amount of alcohol I had consumed over the past few days, but I suppose I was still excited about my move to London and was still on a bit of a high. After I figured out which platform to go to, I waited on my train to take me out to Liverpool Street, where I would face the music again.

Chapter 10

Getting Sacked and Signing on the Sick

I arrived at the job on good time and just continued on what I was doing the day before, which was very little, mostly walking about with a yard brush in my hand. It was near lunchtime when Mick arrived and I knew from the way he looked at me that he wasn't too pleased to see me. When he asked a few of the other lads beside me to go for a pint, and ignored me, I knew my days in my new job where numbered. But I needed a drink myself, so I headed off on my own to the first pub I met. After a few pints I went back to the job as I still wasn't in the form for eating.

After me and Mick exchanged a few funny looks at each other, he finally approached and said, 'That was some aggro last night.' I nodded in agreement. He then asked if I remembered much about it. I said I remembered everything about it and I wouldn't forget his wife ordering me out of their house in the middle of the night. He says, 'If you think that's bad, she put me out as well and I ended up sleeping in the shed.' That probably explained his shabby appearance and I couldn't help but laugh at the whole experience.

I went to work on Saturday and Sunday and nobody seemed to bother or care what I was doing. I didn't bother going to work on Monday, as I was going to meet my brother Edmund who was on his way to London. I was also going to have a look at a room in a house in North Acton that I was interested in renting. Frank told me I would be elected if I got in there as it was a great house for parties. So, after meeting my brother, I then went and met with the three girls who were already living in the house that was soon to become my digs. I took the room and moved my stuff in. Needless to say, my stuff was easy moved as I always travelled light. A previous occupant of the house had left a sleeping bag behind, so I opened it up and just used it as a duvet cover.

Two mates of mine also moved into the house so there was now six of us sharing. The house itself was a large, three storey building and the ground floor was occupied by a 24 hour mini cab service. This would prove to be both good and bad later on. On Tuesday morning, I travelled back down with Edmund to the office in Shepherds Bush.

Edmund wanted to see about getting a job and I had intended on going on out to my job in Liverpool Street. Mick, my foreman, was also there but he had other ideas and when he saw me, he told me that I was sacked for taking Monday off without asking him. Part of me was mad but I also felt relieved as I knew it was only a matter of time before something else went wrong.

Edmund got started on a job. But I decided I needed a few days off as I wanted to register with a doctor, to see if I would qualify for disability benefit and maybe get my rent paid as well. I managed to get an appointment with a doctor whose surgery was a few doors down from my digs. I had letters with me from my own solicitor and doctor in Ireland, detailing the extent of my injuries. After examining me, my doctor suggested that I would be much better off staying in Ireland as he couldn't understand what brought me to London in the first place. I explained that I needed a change as I was about to crack up and also thought I might get better physiotherapy. I also explained that the change would do me good. Eventually, he gave me a cert declaring me unfit for work for one month.

After that, I made my way down to my local DHSS office and made my claim. The girl who was interviewing me was more than understanding and, after hearing my very sad life story, said I would qualify for a counter payment. That was what I had been hoping, because as well as receiving some money (which I badly needed) it also meant that my claim was granted and I would receive my payments on a fortnightly basis. I also had a letter from my landlord stating how much rent I was paying, so the next morning I went up to Ealing, to the Housing Benefit Department and made my claim for rent allowance.

I felt good now that I had all that business sorted out and I also noticed that I was getting much stronger and fitter on my feet, due to all the walking and rushing to catch tubes and buses. I was also getting more familiar with the underground.

I went back down to the office on Thursday, as I had four days wages to collect. I was sent out to another job, which was also beside Liverpool Street tube station. That suited me fine as I could get the Central Line direct from North Acton. Things were looking good once again. This time I was labouring to a concrete gang, the work was heavy but, after I got over the first week, I was becoming more and more able for it. After I collected my first full week's wages, I decided I would check out the Windmill pub on Acton High Street, as I was told that was where all the lads from home drank and it was the place for the craic.

Chapter 11

My First Party

Later that night in the Windmill pub, I got talking to three girls. When I told them where I was living, they said they had heard it was a great house for parties and that I should let them know when the next one was taking place. Well, I thought I would play my innocent part again and asked them to explain exactly what they thought a good party was, as I was only new in town. They said, you just listen to some music, have a drink and maybe a dance and whatever. So I suggested that we should have one of these parties right away as I was anxious to find out what whatever might turn out to be.

At closing time we formed a kitty and bought a good, big carry out. Back at my house we got the music blaring and were dancing on tables, chairs and just going crazy around the house. It wasn't too long until we had everybody else in the house awake. Somehow, I managed to go to work the next morning and after I got the shift finished I made my way back to the Windmill. Later that night, the landlady approached me and asked if my name Martin Jim. I said it was. She told me that she heard I was very wild back at home and was wondering if that was true. I then asked her her name and she said, 'You can call me Amy.' I then replied, 'Yes, Amy, it's true. I was wild back at home and guess what? I'm still fucking wild.'

She said she didn't care what people said about me as she thought she was going to like me. After our introduction, we had a drink and became really good friends and on several occasions, later, she helped me out when I was skint and needed the sub. She also got me a job with a brewery. I really was enjoying my new lease of life. It felt great to be back at work. My social life was also on the up and I now had money and could go anywhere. The craic was good and, as of yet, I still wasn't barred from any pubs in London. When I first decided to come to London, all I wanted to do was to get enough money to survive and enjoy myself, as I still had my compensation claim to look forward to, whenever that might be.

One of the girls I was sharing the house with advised me to save enough money for the fare home as, she said, 'you never knew when that might be'. It was good advice but somehow I never managed it, and only for so many good friends and family I would not be here today.

After a few weeks shovelling and wheeling concrete I began to hit form but I also seemed to be drinking much more. We were going to the pub lunchtime and most evenings after work as well. It wasn't long before I started missing shifts and turning up in the mornings really hungover. One Friday morning, instead of going to work, I decided I would go out to Luton and meet up with a few mates who were living there. The night before I had borrowed £50 from my work mate, Pat, so I thought I had better square up my debt first. I arrived out on the job about 10 a.m. wearing my best clothes and was met by Drew, our foreman, who asked me if I knew what time it was. I told him I had no intention of starting work and only came out as I wanted to see Pat. Drew asked me to stay to dump a load of concrete, which had already started to go hard. He said if I did that, I could then go and he would put me in for the full shift. Pat also asked me to stay and offered to give me a helping hand. So a few hours later and soaking in my own sweat, I was on the train to Luton.

Chapter 12

My First Time in an Airport

I managed to make it out to the job on Monday morning but I was feeling wrecked after my weekend drinking out in Luton. So I didn't stay for the full shift. Needless to say, that night ended up in another big session. Tuesday and Wednesday were pretty much the same. When I opened my wages on Thursday, I noticed that I had been docked so I was feeling really pissed off with Drew about it, even though I was in the wrong and knew I was messing him about. I had heard from another mate that had worked on a site nearby that there was a good pub near us that had strippers and played good music during the day. At lunchtime I suggested to Pat and another lad called Enda that we should go there for a pint. The three of us had just approached the bar when we were met by the first stripper. She was holding a pint tumbler, half full of pound coins, so we soon added three more.

We were just beginning to enjoy our pints, when we were approached by the second stripper who, after teasing us with her assets, relieved us of another three pounds. There were three strippers working and, at the pace they were approaching us, I knew it couldn't last much longer. Enda suggested a few times that we just should leave. It was only six weeks to Christmas and he didn't want to lose his job. I didn't know what was going through Pat's mind but I was delighted when he ordered three more pints. Once again, we were approached by one of our lady friends but this time I just put a ten pence coin into her collection. She was furious with me and demanded, 'Do you not think I'm worth more than that?' I said she probably was and threw a two pence coin into her glass. For a second I thought she was going to hit me with the tumbler but she was speechless. Then Enda threw in another ten pence coin. After staring into the tumbler in disbelief for a few seconds, she then started yelling at us and called over the bouncers to remove us. As we were leaving, Enda was pointing towards the tumbler and asked, 'Who the fuck put the penny in?'

On the way back to work, myself and Pat were laughing at the craic but Enda seemed anxious about his job. Once we did get on site Enda said he was going to speak with Drew, as he wanted to know if he could finish work a little bit earlier, as he wanted to go into the office in Shepherds Bush to sort out a mistake in his wages. When he explained this to Drew, Drew said it wouldn't be a problem. But to our shock, Drew then told him not to bother coming back as he was sacked. On hearing this and seeing the expression on Enda's face, I just burst into laughter. Drew then turned to me and asked what I thought was funny about it as I was also sacked, and that we should take Pat with us on our way out. After hearing that I didn't think it was as funny. All I could think about at that moment was the morning I was on my way to Luton and started working, wearing my good clothes and later getting docked in my wages.

I started swearing at Drew and followed him into his office as he tried to get away from me. I had a hold of him by the throat and he was telling me to settle down and agreed to give me a new time sheet to take into the office. Well I did calm down and after Drew wrote me out my new time sheet, with all the extra hours I made my way back into the office. I presented them with it and told them there was a mistake in my wages. I did get paid for the full week, but was later told that they knew I was one hundred per cent in the wrong and that I should apologise to Drew. I did mean to apologise to Drew as I knew he was only doing his job and I did like him. He was a decent bloke.

I was now looking forward to a long weekend off as I had qualified for both disability benefit and rent allowance. Things were looking bright for me once again.

After partying all weekend, I got a phone call from my solicitor on Monday morning, telling me I had to be in Dublin for 11am the following morning, for an appointment and a medical check-up with the insurance company. It wasn't the news I had wanted to hear because, as well as being really hungover, I had never flown before. So this was going to be a new experience for me. After a quick shower, I threw a few things into my bag and headed for Heathrow.

I arrived at Heathrow Airport, nervous and excited and craving for a drink. I approached a girl at an Aer Lingus desk and explained my situation. When I told her that I had never flown before, she had the nerve to ask me how I got here in the first place. I replied back by asking her, did she ever hear of a thing called a boat? Well, after all the confusion, I purchased a return ticket to Dublin. I decided I would get the last flight out of Dublin the following day, as that would give me plenty of time after my check-up. After I got my luggage checked in I made my way to the bar and ordered a double brandy with a dash of port. After knocking that straight back, I then had three more, so for now, I was well cured. My nerves had settled and I was now looking forward to the rest of my journey. I also got talking to another couple who were getting the same flight as me, so I just sort of followed them and assumed they knew what they were doing. On the short flight to Dublin I managed to consume a few more quick brandies. I was in top form as I booked myself into a B&B on Gardiner St. After eating what was to be my only meal that day, I then went on a pub crawl around Dublin city centre. That night I ended up in a disco on Harcourt Street, called Copper Face Jacks.

Chapter 13

Going on a Bender

The next morning I awoke with another serious hangover and, after a quick shower and a very light breakfast, I decided I would walk to the Mater Private Hospital for my appointment. I was hoping the walk might clear my head a bit and also that the fresh air would do me good. I was craving for a drink but decided I would suffer until after my appointment. When the Doctor finally called me into his office, he told me to get undressed and hop up on the couch and he would have a look at me. I took my time and, after struggling with my clothes and complaining about the pain, I finally got up on his couch. After a quick examination, the doctor told me I was a very lucky man. I asked him how he figured that one out. He said, with the extent of my injuries I was lucky to be so well. I snapped back at him by saying he was the lucky one as it didn't happen to him. I don't think he thought I was very funny so, after another struggle getting dressed I left, and hobbled down the street out of sight and into the first pub I came to. After getting the cure, I spent the rest of the day in Dublin going from pub to pub, before making my way back out to the airport to get my flight back to London.

The next day I went drinking again with another mate called Pete. After we got pissed out of our minds, we decided we should head to Soho for a drink to see what the craic was there. The first club we went into was empty, apart from a huge man who very quickly asked us what we were looking for. When we told him we wanted more drink and some nice female company, he then invited us to follow him upstairs to meet with some girls who 'would sort us out'. At the top of the stairs we were introduced to a lady who explained what was on offer and what each service cost. I asked if I could use their toilet while I would think about it.

I wasn't too long in the toilet, when I heard the commotion and a row breaking out on the landing between Pete and the bouncer/pimp. So when I got out I was asked to leave and take my mate with me. Once outside the door, I found Pete lying on the street complaining of a sore knee. He was laughing and asked me how I got on. I told him that I didn't get on at all. The police arrived, but when I said we were leaving as soon as we got a taxi they seemed to be happy enough with that.

Getting a taxi proved to be very difficult as the black taxis would not go outside of the square mile. Eventually, I managed to hail down a mini cab that brought us back to Acton. For the next three days, Pete and myself continued on our drinking binge while all the time Pete was complaining about his sore knee.

On Saturday evening, we were having another party in a friend's house when I decided I should phone for an ambulance for Pete, who seemed to be in severe pain. After phoning for the ambulance I then rang for a mini cab for myself as I thought I would head down to a pub in Acton. My taxi arrived before the ambulance and, needless to say, Pete hobbled out and into the taxi with me. When we arrived at the pub the landlord refused to serve us. So, while Pete waited outside the door, I went across the street into a phone box and rang for another ambulance. I told Pete to stay where he was, as the ambulance was on its way. I said goodbye and good luck and then headed off walking up the street towards another pub that I figured I would get served in. I hadn't gone too far when I heard Pete swearing and shouting at me to wait for him. Well, I soon turned back and put my arm around him and between staggering and swearing and laughing, we fell into another pub. This time we did get served as it was a bar where all the hard drinkers and characters drank in. After a few more rounds of drink and listening to Pete complaining about his sore knee, I rang for the third time and ordered another ambulance. The good news was that we did wait for this ambulance. We were happy enough as long as we were both getting served but the bad news was that Pete's knee had been badly broken all that time.

I heard later that the police called at the house where I had rang for the first ambulance, so I was probably very lucky I wasn't arrested for wasting their time and making hoax calls. I did genuinely want an ambulance every time I rang but we just didn't have the patience or sobriety to wait for it. Pete was admitted to hospital for a few days, where he had a plaster fitted to his leg and he eventually made a full recovery.

After going on another bender, on my own, all day Sunday, I awoke on Monday morning early and made my way down to the office again. I was wrecked and was a lot worse for wear after my binge on the drink. This time I got sent to a job which was near Oxford Circus tube station. Somehow, I managed to keep it until Christmas.

I hadn't planned on going home for Christmas but my mate, Frank, called up at my house and asked me to come with him as he was taking his car. Another mate, Paul, was coming with us so, the day before Christmas Eve, the three of us set off on the journey with a bottle of vodka each and a good supply of tins of lager. We were in high spirits on the boat as we met up with a lot of other lads from home. The drinks were coming up fast and furious and I don't know how long we were sailing when the barman decided to close the bar. He had given us all a couple of warnings earlier to quieten down, which we didn't take any heed of. We were mostly just messing about and bantering with each other. In hindsight, it was probably a good decision as it could easily have gotten out of hand and ended up in a boxing match. I don't know how Frank managed to drive but, after leaving the boat, he took the wrong exit off a roundabout and instead of heading for Donegal, we eventually ended up in Bangor, Co. Down.

We decided we would book into a B&B for the night but, after being refused in the first two places, we finally got into a hotel. That night we ended up at a disco in the town. I remember a big fight breaking out but luckily we were not involved. We did make it home the following night, after checking out endless bars on our way. After that I had a quiet Christmas and New Year at home in Carrigart and thought it would be a good idea to cut down on my drinking when I would go back to London.

For the next two months or so I drifted in and out between jobs, but I was still drinking very heavily and, if I wasn't getting sacked, I would just walk off the job or not bother going at all. Sometimes, I would last to breakfast or maybe lunchtime. I remember, at least twice, just clocking in and walking straight back out again. Also, if I knew anybody on the job with the same craving for drink as I had, I would try and talk them into joining me.

I remember one day I was sent out to a job in Windsor and was working alongside two men – one from Co. Cork and one from London. We very soon got talking about my favourite subject at that time, which was drink, so at lunchtime I suggested we would go for a pint. Well, as usual, one led to two and then three and so on and it wasn't very long until we were in great spirits. Myself and the fellow from Co. Cork were singing as loud as we could, while stamping our feet on the ground and hitting the table an odd hard thump for good measure. Needless to say, the landlord asked us to leave and not bother coming back. My new drinking buddy from Co. Cork then replied by saying that we would be happy to leave his pub, when they left our country. Our other drinking mate from London, was disgusted with us and approached the landlord and apologised on his own behalf, by saying he was sorry as he didn't know the kind of us. Well, me and my Co. Cork buddy were not too happy on hearing that, as he didn't seem to have a problem accepting our drink earlier and in fact let us do the bulk of the buying. My mate from Co. Cork threw a pint of beer over him, while I took aim and tried to catch him with a right hook. We quickly made our escape before heading back to the job.

It was almost 5pm and we were hoping we would get a lift back into London in the work van, but as soon as our foreman saw us he told us to get lost. As we turned to leave, I shouted to him not to forget to put us in for a half day's wages. Making our way to get a train back into London, Co. Cork (I can't remember my buddy's name) explained then he didn't have any money left to buy a ticket! I had enough left for two tickets, but said we would chance it and we could have another few drinks when we would get closer to home. The train was packed and we were not too long into our journey when we were approached by two ticket inspectors. I was trying to explain that it was my first time on a train and that I thought you just paid at the end of your journey. I was really acting up my wee innocent role again and had just produced the money to purchase two tickets, when a big American tourist spoke up and said, 'Arrest those two guys.'

Well, that was all it needed to start another handling. Co. Cork jumped from his seat and, grabbing the American by the throat, told him it was none of his business. Luckily, we were just approaching some station at that time, so through all the mayhem I managed to make escape alone. I did manage to make it back to North Acton tube station that night, without a ticket and that was the last I seen or heard of Co. Cork.

Chapter 14

Three More Appointments with the Insurance Company – Missing the First One

The following Friday I received another call from my solicitor. This time they wanted me home for three more appointments with doctors, acting on behalf of the insurance company. The first appointment was for Monday morning in Letterkenny and the other two were in Dublin on the following day. I had been on a continuous bender. I had acquired a lot of hard drinking friends and there was never a shortage of flats or houses to visit if you needed a drink or wanted somebody to go to the pub with. I had often heard the old saying that you would get money for drink when you couldn't get it for anything else and it definitely seemed like that back then.

On Sunday morning, I packed my bag once again but figured I could afford a few drinks and the fare home, so my first stop was the Windmill Pub. I wasn't very long in the Windmill, when I knew I had dipped into my ticket money so, instead of facing up to the predicament I was now in; I headed next door to the Blarney Stone, where I knew a live band would be playing. I continued on drinking there until around 10pm before getting a taxi up to the Galtymore Nite Club in Cricklewood, with my mate, Alan.

It was one of those days when you can drink yourself sober again and after the band had stopped playing, I went up to the food bar for a chicken and chip supper. I now had five pounds left. A girl then came up and stood beside me and after placing her order we got talking. She told me she was from London and living in Ealing. When I asked her for her full address, she asked me why I wanted it. I told her I was after finishing a wild binge on the drink and knew I wasn't going to be able to sleep for the next couple of days or nights so, if I had her address, I would write her nice love letters to help me pass my time. After looking at me for a moment or two, she just burst out laughing and asked the girl serving us for a pen and a piece of paper. After writing down her details, she handed the piece of paper to me. It was a serviette. At this stage I had just finished eating my chip supper and, after wiping my face with her addressed serviette, I then threw it over the counter. I apologised and after receiving another addressed serviette, I did exactly the same thing. This time my friend just walked away and left me standing alone at the counter. I was sure now I had blown my chances.

Once outside, I noticed a bicycle sitting alongside a railing. However, what I failed to notice was the chain and padlock attached to it. As I attempted to mount the bicycle I then felt a tap on my shoulder. I was certain it was the police, or whoever owned the bicycle, and was so relieved when I discovered it was my lady friend, who asked me if I would like to come to a party in her house in Ealing. Things were looking bright once again, well at least for the time being, and I figured the five pounds in my pocket would still get me back to Acton the next day. I also decided I would try and forget about my appointments in Ireland and would worry about them at a later date.

Back in the party house we were joined by another couple and I insisted on buying some drink as I didn't like coming to a party empty handed. My lady friend then walked up the street with me where I managed to purchase four cans of lager at one pound each. Back in the house, I explained to the other couple that I was after making a huge decision – should I buy four cans and get the bus home in the morning or five cans and walk it? My date's friend told me that her fellow and my woman would both be going to work in the morning so, after that, me and her would go for a good drink. That also sounded like a good idea at the time, as she was a very attractive woman and I knew we would click big time. Well, I don't think I got any sleep at all that night. But I do remember looking out the window as morning broke and beginning to panic with reality sinking in. Here I was in Ealing, on Monday morning, with a one pound coin to my name, when I should have been in Letterkenny for the first of my appointments.

Well, I shouted goodbye and good luck as I headed out the door in a hurry, without explaining the predicament I had gotten myself into. I decided I would also walk the whole way back to Acton and by that stage the rest of my housemates would be at work. It meant I wouldn't have to talk to them and could just go to bed and get some sleep, as I was completely wrecked. When I finally arrived at my house, my mate, Joe, was still there. He laughed when he saw the state I was in. He said, 'I thought you went home yesterday,' and I said, 'Don't ask, it's a long story.' He then asked if I had any money. I knew what he meant but I said, 'Sure, I can give you a pound if you're stuck.' We both laughed at that. Joe would have known I was broke. After getting a sub from Joe for £250, I threw some cold water over my face, changed my shirt and headed, once again, for Heathrow. This time I had no bag to pack, as it was still lying in the Windmill from the day before. I figured out that, even though I had missed my first appointment, all going well, I would still manage to make it to the other two the following day in Dublin.

Chapter 15

Getting Arrested on the Journey Home

After arriving at Heathrow and buying a return ticket to Dublin, I went straight to the bar as I needed a couple of drinks to calm my nerves. I was beginning to go into the horrors and was feeling very paranoid. I also noticed my shirt was all creased as it hadn't been ironed. I ordered a triple brandy with a dash of port. My hands were shaking so bad as I tried to raise the glass to my mouth. I held the glass with both hands and made my way towards the corner of the bar where it was quiet. There I managed to get it swallowed in one go. After ordering the same again and getting it into me, I could feel a hot flush hitting me and I started to relax. I was talking and praying to myself and promising St Anthony that if he got me through this siege safe and well, I would give up the drink.

I was seated next to a woman on the plane and during the flight I started going into the horrors once again. I could hear voices in my head and thought that there were people coming to give me a thumping. I was now so frightened and felt so alone. I was wishing I had someone with me, as I knew I had a bad journey in front of me. One of the air hostesses must have noticed my state of panic because she approached me and asked me if I was ok. I thought I would play my innocent role again and, as I wanted as much help and sympathy as I could get, I told her I was after getting very bad news from home – both my parents had been out on a boat and had got lost at sea. After sympathising with me, she then asked if she could get me anything. I said I would love a large brandy. Holding the glass again with both my hands, I tried to raise it to my mouth but this time I was shaking so bad I couldn't hold it and spilled it over the lady next to me. She called the air hostess over again and asked to get moved to a different seat, which made me feel twice as paranoid. I did try to apologise but she just ignored me and, as she got out of her seat, she wiped my good brandy from her clothes. I was thinking about that episode later and I didn't feel as bad about it because, as far as that lady was concerned, I was on my way home to a terrible tragedy and she didn't even have the manners to offer me her sympathy.

After getting off the plane, I made my way into Dublin city centre. I had now decided I would get a bus back up home and travel down again in the morning as it would be a lot safer for me than spending the night in Dublin. I was also hoping that once I got seated on the bus, I would get some badly needed sleep. I had another two hours to wait until my bus would leave, so I knew I couldn't sit in the one place for too long. I started walking around Dublin city centre in a sort of a circle. Passing a shoe shop, I decided I would buy myself a pair of runners as I was wearing a big pair of heavy black shoes. I wanted something cheap and light so, after making my purchase, I started on my way with what I thought were my new runners.

Walking as hard as I could, I thought I noticed people staring at my feet but at first I just put it down to paranoia. It was only after some time, when my feet started to burn, that I looked down and realised I was walking around Dublin in a pair of bedroom slippers. It was luck that I still had my shoes with me in a carrier bag so, after quickly changing back into them, I threw my bedroom slippers over the bridge and into the Liffey River.

I now made my way to get my bus and, en route, I decided to buy a bottle of mouthwash as the inside of my mouth smelled just as bad as the slippers I had been wearing. I spilled some and swallowed the rest of the mouthwash before I hopped on my bus for Donegal. I sat at the rear, hoping I would doze off, but again I felt myself going into the horrors, hearing all these crazy voices in my head. I rushed up to the driver and asked him to put a few men off the bus, as my life was in danger. He told me to get back into my seat as I was annoying him and everybody else on the bus. I then sat next to two old ladies and began telling them about my accident. I was talking fairly loud as I wanted everyone to hear my sad story and was secretly hoping that somebody would have sympathy for me and save me.

When we stopped in Co. Monaghan for a fifteen-minute break, I kept close to the two women. I knew they couldn't save me, but at least I would have witnesses who could inform my family and let them know what hospital I was taken to, or whatever. I was a nervous wreck and kept hearing voices in my head. The voices were men who wanted to attack me and beat me up. For the remainder of our journey from Monaghan to Letterkenny I kept on moving from seat to seat as I was afraid to fall asleep. As the bus was pulling into the depot in Letterkenny, I was standing at the front and, once the doors opened, I made a run for it up the street as fast as I could go. I was looking over my shoulder every so often, to see if I was being followed. As I reached a café, I decided I would be safer in it, so I ran in the door and scrambled over the counter. One of the girls who was working there must have sensed that I was suffering from the horrors. She kept talking to me and telling me that I was safe and after getting me a seat she then gave me a cup of tea.

The Gardaí arrived on the scene before I had time to either drink it or spill it and, after placing me in the back seat of the patrol car, they brought me to the Garda Station. It was probably the first time I was glad to get arrested, as I felt safe. I don't know how long I was there but when they phoned my brother, I started shouting down the phone. I was telling him to bring a gun with him as I was under pressure.

My brother did come and lift me and we made our way home to Carrigart. I ranted and raved most of that night and was still suffering from the horrors the following morning, as we set off on our journey back down to Dublin for my two appointments. My brother and his wife took their car and I lay down across the back seat hoping I would sleep.

Chapter 16

My Second Appointment with the Insurance Board – Getting Kicked Out

We arrived in good time for my first appointment in the Blackrock Clinic. It was with a urologist as I had told them I had lost all interest in sex as a result of my accident. After waiting for ages, I finally got called in. They examined all around my 'private area' and asked me all sorts of personal questions which I knew I answered quite well. The doctor then produced a universal container and asked me for a sample of my sperm. I was expecting him to look for that so I had treated myself first thing in the morning, before I left the house. As I was now preparing to give my sample, I was looking around the toilet to see if there were any cameras installed. I was taking my time and twisting up my face as if it was hurting me, just in case he was sitting watching my performance on a screen. What I didn't realise, though, was that I was now going to be late for my second appointment.

My brother, Eunan, and his wife, Nancy, were waiting out in the car for me, and as we made our way to Fitzwilliam Square for my second showdown, Nancy asked how I got on. Even though I was still in really bad form, I still had my good sense of humour and told her I was just like the 'wee genie' as I was after coming in a bottle as well! I don't know how late I was when I got as far as my next appointment and when I told the lady at the reception desk my name and the name of the doctor I was to see, she told me there was no such person. I explained that was the name that was on my letter and when she asked me for the letter, I realised they still had it in Blackrock Clinic. I had figured that, as they were both acting on behalf of the insurance company, they were just trying to confuse me and see how I would react. She then suggested that she should phone my solicitor to clarify the matter but I suggested that she should phone Blackrock Clinic instead, as it would only cost her the price of a local call. When she then told me not to tell her what to do, I snapped back by saying, 'Don't you try and fuck me about.' She began walking briskly down a corridor, with me in full swing behind her. She told me she wasn't going to listen while I was swearing at her. She then passed an open door and pointed towards it, signalling for me to enter. I was halfways in the door when a man who looked near retiring age shouted at me to close the door behind me. I shouted back, 'Wait until I get fucking in first.'

At this stage I was just totally shattered and was about to explode. The doctor introduced himself and after getting off to a very bad start, our meeting then went completely out of control. Anything he said I disagreed with, as I thought he was totally wrong. He then showed me all the letters after his name and asked who the hell I thought I was to be contradicting him. 'Do you think I am just an odd job man. I know what I am talking about,' he said. Well, I replied back by telling him I also knew what he was talking and it was just a load of bullshit. He removed his glasses and hit the table a thump with his fist and roared at me to get out. I was tempted to take a swing at him but I was so exhausted, both physically and mentally, that I would probably just have dropped at his feet. In his report to my solicitor, he said that I was very aggressive and suggested I should be referred to a psychiatrist. My solicitor said the referral to the shrink might work out in my favour as it could be said that my aggression was a direct result of my accident.

Chapter 17

A Brief Stint in Kew Gardens

As I didn't know when my next appointment might be, I headed back to London once again. Only I was still receiving disability benefit and rent allowance I wouldn't have managed to survive. After dossing about for the next week, I went back down to 'the office'. This time I got sent out to a job in Kew Gardens. I was able to get the train directly from Acton Central Station. The first month passed off without any bother. I wasn't drinking much but once I got my debt paid back to Joe I went off on another bender. I missed a few days at work but did go back again as I was getting on well with my foreman.

As always, I was trying to dodge paying the train fare. I would just pay for one stop but if the coast was clear, I would pay nothing. One evening they were waiting for me and as I handed over my forty pence the inspector asked me where I had come from. I was caught unawares and couldn't think of the name of the previous stop. I was trying to buy time as I was trying to remember the name so I replied back by saying that I came from Ireland. I don't know what nationality he was but in very broken English he says, "No, no, no. I mean where you come from here?" I was now enjoying the craic as I knew I was confusing him, so I then replied by saying that I was sorry and that I misunderstood the question. I continued to explain that I was from Ealing and that I was missing my family back at home. I really had got him flustered at this stage and, as he raised his hands in sheer frustration, I suddenly remembered the name of the station and so told them that I had travelled from Gunnersbury. But what I didn't know was that the fares had increased so, after paying the extra money, I got on my way. Meanwhile, the Inspector was pointing his finger at me and saying, 'You Irish are crazy.'

As usual, I didn't last much longer in my new job. One Saturday, Marty, my foreman, asked me to take him up on a cherry picker as he wanted to check out something on the roof. He explained that it wouldn't take us long and we could finish up early. At that time it wasn't a good idea to put me in charge of any mechanical vehicle considering my fondness of the bottle. So what Marty didn't realise that day was that I had consumed quite a few brandies on my lunch break. We both got into the cage and I seemed to be managing the controls ok on our way up. As I tried to get positioned close to the rooftop, Marty must have sensed, or indeed smelled, something as he asked me how many drinks I had. I told him I had lost count so now he began to panic. He told me to move over and he would take control and take us down again. I told him that as I was good enough to get us up I would sure enough be good enough to take us down again. I was now feeling more drunk and was also laughing at Marty's expression as he shouted at me to let go of the controls. I did manage to get us down but not without smashing a few panes of glass in the process. It was a massive greenhouse. I walked away from the job that afternoon and got my train back into Acton. That was my last time in Kew Gardens.

Chapter 18

More Drink and Even More Craic

That night I was involved in another accident and was lucky to escape without serious injury. After being refused entry to a nightclub, myself and a mate then went to a club nearby that only black people went into. It was located behind a fish market. The only reason I knew it existed was that one morning I noticed people coming out, stoned out of their heads. Even though we got a few funny looks at first and were the only two white people in the place, nobody gave us any bother. After we left, and as we tried to make our way back to my house, I staggered out in front of an oncoming car and was knocked into the air. Somehow I managed to escape from that unharmed or without any broken bones, so St. Anthony had saved me once again.

I didn't bother looking for any work the following week as myself and my mate were on a serious bender. We could buy drink from an off-licence beside my house at all hours, so as soon as we awoke in the morning we would buy a few bottles of cider and some cans of extra strength lager. That was my first time getting introduced to snakebites and we used to be out of our heads at normal pub opening hours. In fact we were just topping up from the previous night's session. Some days we would eat nothing at all and just continue drinking, while most days there would be an incident of some sort or another. We were either trying to get out of taxis, tubes or buses without paying or getting barred from some pub.

One day, while we were walking up a street in Peckham, my mate lifted a rocking chair from outside a furniture shop. I don't know how he intended on taking it on the tube but we got caught before we got that far. We were taking it in turns to carry it and I was almost certain we had got away unnoticed, as we seemed to be walking for ages. We were also taking it in turns to sit on it, but eventually we were confronted by the owners who were Pakistanis. They threatened to shoot us if we put up any fight at all. Well, we soon left down the chair after that and even though I could picture the chair in my living room we figured it wasn't worth getting shot over.

The following day after our breakfast of Snakebites, I figured that if we got on the 266 bus in Horn Lane we could visit the Three Crowns pubs – the first one was in Harlesden, the second in Willesden and the third in Cricklewood. We did manage a few drinks in all three and our session finished up in the Archway Tavern on Holloway Road.

That weekend my two house mates told me they had taken a job in Harlesden and they needed a labourer, if I was interested. I told them I was, so we arranged a time for Monday morning. This sounded good as I had a lift from my house straight to the job and back again. Things were looking bright once again.

On Monday morning, the three of us landed on the job so my task was to keep them in concrete for the day. I was flat out filling the mixer and wheeling my mix to the lads and everything was going ok. I was soaking in my own sweat but was happy, as I wanted to get back in good form again and knew if I could stick it out that after a few days I would be ok. There was a shop next door to our job and there was a huge Alsatian patrolling the backyard, just bordering where we were working. It growled at us from the moment we started but we figured that we were safe enough as it couldn't get out through the wooden fencing. When I arrived at the site I made a gesture with my shovel at her, indicating that she should not come near me or else! But every time I wheeled the wheelbarrow past a certain part of the fence, which I should point out was partly broken, she was there pulling at it determined to get loose and show us who was boss. Initially we thought we were safe as we didn't realise the fence was damaged. But now we weren't so sure. Shortly after lunchtime, as I was filling the mixer, I heard one of the lads shouting at us to run. As I looked up, I could see that our friend had eventually managed to break free. Ironically, all morning I had been winding the lads up saying there were working me too hard and that I had very bad leg injuries. But once our friend got loose and came after us I passed out my two mates as we made our escape. My mates jumped into their car and closed the doors but I just kept on going as I could see a pub door opening in front of me. When I knew I was safe and after a few double brandies, I thought for a few moments about my escape and the speed of it. I had surprised myself at how fast I had run. It's possible the Alsatian didn't even chase after us as I didn't even bother looking over my shoulder. After my run and my morning's work, not to mention the previous week's drinking, I felt absolutely wrecked. So going back to work was the last thing on my mind.

I now wanted more drink but I was almost broke, so I decided I would go down to my local in Acton and ask the landlady for a sub. I had the price of a pint left so after Amy had served me I picked up the courage and asked her if there was any chance of a sub. She asked me how much I wanted so I said I would need £50. She said that if she gave me £50 now I wouldn't bother going to work the following day. So she handed me £25 and told me to return the following day for the final installment. But I then said to her, 'Jesus, Amy, If you don't give me the £50 now I will have to take tomorrow off and come in again for the other £25,' to which she replied, 'I suppose you're right,' and she then handed me the £50. I thanked her and told her I would pay her back as soon as I could. 'I know you will,' she says, 'Otherwise I wouldn't have given it to you.'

I never bothered going to work the next day and my two housemates had to get another labourer. On the Friday I was still dossing and was walking near my house when a fierce thunder shower started. I had taken my shirt off earlier, as it was very warm, so once again I started to run as fast as I could go. I had my head down and who should I run into but my doctor. I almost knocked him to the ground so I just kept on going and didn't even take the time to apologise. Back up at the house, I knew I was in a predicament. How could I look for another sick cert? I was using my leg injury as my main reason for being unable to work. After thinking about it for a few minutes I rang the surgery and asked the girl at reception for an appointment. I explained that it was very urgent and that I was in an awful lot of pain. She told me she had a cancellation and that I should just come on down.

When the time came to face the music, I put on my 'poor me' act. I limped in through the door while at the same time let out a few screeches indicating that I was in severe agony. Straight away my doctor asked if it was me that had run into him earlier. I said, 'maybe it was' and continued on by telling him that I was out for a walk and when the rain started, I was rushing back to the house and when I was almost at the top of the stairs, my legs just went numb and gave way. I explained that I had fallen down the stairs and needed some painkillers or an injection as my back was killing me. He was reluctant at the outset to give me anything but I managed to get a prescription and another sick cert for one more month. When I moved into my house I thought it was great to be so close to the surgery but now I wasn't so sure. I also knew that I would have trouble getting another cert from him, so I figured that I needed to change my doctor pretty soon.

Most of my hard drinking buddies were also claiming disability benefits so the very next week I was introduced to a very good doctor, who was from Pakistan. He had a great understanding for my situation and had a lot of sympathy for me, so I got registered at his surgery. It was a huge relief knowing that I didn't have to go back to my own doctor again. When I was due my next cert my doctor asked how long I needed it for, so I told him that three months would do me for now. I was still dossing and still consuming large amounts of alcohol. I often compared my digs at Horn Lane to a train station. There were always different people coming and going and it was the house for anybody and everybody to have a party in.

One Sunday night I was at yet another party. This time it was in a house in Shepherds Bush within walking distance to the work office. The party was still going strong on Monday morning when I decided I should go down and see Leo the boss, and hopefully get started back at work. As usual, there was a large group of men gathered outside, all different nationalities and all looking for work. When Leo saw me approaching, he burst out laughing and said, 'Don't tell me you're looking for work.' Well, I replied back by saying that work was the last thing on my mind but I wanted him to send me out on a job where I could just doss about and still get a wage packet at the end of the week. Leo looked me up and down and asked, 'Are you sure you don't need anything else?' 'Well,' I said, 'Seeing as you are asking, there is one other thing. I wouldn't mind a job near a pub and also near a tube.' We had an audience listening in at this stage, so Leo asked if that was all. I replied back by saying, 'Well, I would like a few of my mates on the job with me as it's not much craic drinking on your own,' to which he replied, 'Is it a day's work or a fucking party you're after?' He then called over one of his foremen and said, 'take this head case with you.'

Leo was one very good mate who was always there for me when I needed him. He was probably the only man in London that morning that would have started me on a job because, as well as still wearing my party clothes, I was drunk out of my mind. I never bothered asking Leo where or what job we were going to but as I got out of the van onto the site, it all started to look familiar. I had been sent out to a job from which I was sacked a few months earlier. I never bothered speaking to anyone and I just turned and walked away. We were in some part of Rotherhithe so, after finally making my way back to my house, I hopped into bed for some badly needed sleep.

After that I just seemed to go from bad to worse. I remember one week in particular I started and finished in four different jobs. In the first three I only stayed for one day and just didn't bother going back. On the fourth job I managed to go for my second day but went for a drink on my lunch break and never bothered going back. I remember one week Leo sending me out on a job in Earls Court. He said it would suit me good as it was only for three days. The job was almost finished and all I had to do was just tidy up.

On my third and final day, my boss, Pat, told me there were two block and tackles left on the job and that I could take them home with me if I wanted them. I didn't want them myself but figured if I could manage to get them home, I could sell them to my two housemates. At the end of the shift I put both of them into a large bag and got another lad on the job to lift them onto my back. I knew it was going to be a struggle but I was determined to get them home as all I could think about was the handy beer money. I did manage, eventually, to get them home and sold them to my housemates for £15 each but I can tell you, that it was anything but handy. After struggling to get across busy streets, I managed to make it onto the tube, but not before almost crushing the foot of another passenger in the process. When I did arrive into Acton Town tube station, I then had to get myself a taxi so that shaved a bit off my profit.

I remember being sent to another job on Oxford Street and labouring alongside two other lads. One was from Co. Cavan and the other lad was from Australia. Our Aussie mate christened me Paddy 1 and our mate from Co. Cavan was Paddy 2. Myself and Paddy 2 were a bad combination and it wasn't very long until we both got a warning about drinking on the job and timekeeping. In fairness to our ganger man, he was giving us a chance. One lunch break we asked another labourer to join us for a drink. I can't remember which part of the world he came from but he sure was black. So we headed off to the pub, and it was rough, to say the least. It was one of those places where you wouldn't know whether to wipe your boots as you entered or as you left! Well that day we didn't bother going back to the job. We were having too much craic with our friend from Africa or wherever he was from. We were feeding money into a juke box and fighting with our friend about the songs we wanted to listen to. Myself and Paddy 2 wanted Irish songs and our friend wanted reggae music. It was all good craic. At one stage our friend turned to us and said, "You know what Paddys? If I had my good clothes on I wouldn't come in here."

The next morning I went out to the job again but when I met my mate from Australia he told me that Paddy 2 had just been sacked and it wasn't long before I would be following him! Well, true enough the ganger man called me over and said he was sorry, but he had to let me go. When he came onto the job that morning, he found our friend from Africa or wherever, fast asleep in a skip full of rubbish. Well, that was another bad record on my CV, but on my way out I shook hands with everyone and said goodbye to our wee mate from Australia. That was the last time I had seen or heard of any of them and I often wondered what ever happened to Paddy 2.

Living in Acton I used to meet Rhino, the big black guy who starred in the TV show *Gladiators* but we were not on name terms. However, we had our own way of acknowledging each other – he would stand in a pose flexing and showing of his muscles and I would do my party piece of shadow-boxing and dancing around him (just remember I was constantly drunk out of my head during that time). Our friendly banter all came to an end one day when I was walking up to my house. I was full drunk and was wired to the moon. My big friend was standing on the opposite side of the street, so when he saw me he started into his routine. Jesus I was in no form for playing games and so I lost the head and flew into a rage. I was trying to cross a very busy street to get at him, but it was good for me that he ran away laughing.

One other day myself and a mate were walking down Oxford Street. We were just dossing and trying to pass the time. All of a sudden it started to rain very heavily so we just headed in the first door that was open. It happened to be a job centre. We pretended to be interested in the job vacancy adverts. The lady in charge then informed us that it was locking up time but that we should come back again first thing in the morning as their would be more jobs available then. I think she was slightly amused when I replied, 'that's the last fucking thing we will be wanting.'

Chapter 19

Going from Job to Job and Pub to Pub

Back down at the office, Leo sent me to another job. It was in East Grinstead. The foreman seemed to know that I was a bit of a character who was not interested in hard work so he told me he would give me the job of security on the gate. They had a problem with material going missing so it was my responsibility to ensure that all material leaving the site was authorised. It was also a one way system. So I had to stop and ask every vehicle entering who they where and what their errand on the site was. Once I had them checked out, I would then phone the office on the site to see if it was ok for them to drive in, or if they had to wait on a vehicle that might be leaving the site and coming in the opposite direction. Everything went ok for a few days but I was not happy doing it and was getting bored. Also, I did not want the responsibility that was attached to it. One morning I stopped a car and I got the feeling that the occupants were a bit rude. They seemed to think that they were important, as they asked me if I knew who I had just stopped. As it happened, they were both agents on the job. I was told by the office that there was a lorry on its way out but I just told them to keep going as the coast was clear. I then put down the phone and walked off the job.

Shortly after that, one of my drinking buddies asked if I was interested in getting started on a job in Southend. The work would be heavy but well paid. I would get £65 a day and plenty of overtime if I wanted. Well, I did start on that job and the first two weeks were tight going. My tools were a pick and shovel and my hands blistered after the first day. Once I got into my third week I was ok and was able to hold my own. For a while I didn't drink until the weekends, but it just meant I had more money to spend and, with that, a bigger craving for the drink. We worked half days on Saturdays, so a group of us would always go to the pub on our way home for a few drinks. We always had the good intentions of going home and coming back out again, all prepared for a good night on the town.

One Saturday we were in the pub, as usual, in our working gear, enjoying our drinks when a lady, who was seated at a table with her girlfriends, caught my eye. I was very attracted to her so, after we exchanged a few winks, I approached her. I planned my chat up line and went straight for it. So I said to her, 'If I went home, had a shower and a shave, put on a nice aftershave, gelled my hair and put on my best clothes and came back and asked you out, what would you say?' She laughed and said, 'Yes, I would definitely go out with you.' So we exchanged first names and I went back to the bar to finish my drink. I told her I would be back very soon, after my makeover for our date.

When I got back to the bar there were another four drinks waiting for me so, being an alcoholic, I swallowed them down one after the other in very quick succession. I then figured I couldn't leave without buying my round so I ordered one for the road. As much as I wanted to go out with my date, I just couldn't leave my drink so I decided I would approach her again and tell her there was a change of plan. This time I said to her, 'What if I didn't bother going home and asked you out. What would your answer be?' She said her answer would still be the same and suggested I bring over my drink and join her at the table.

It was around this time in my life that I started to develop a very weak bladder. To piss in one's own bed while sleeping alone was bad enough, but to piss the bed belonging to a nice lady friend, whom you were just after meeting, was very embarrassing and not a very good start to any possible relationship. Needless to say we awoke early on Sunday morning and both of us soaked in urine. I had pissed the bed big time. None of us mentioned it and, while my friend was having a well earned shower, I just disappeared out the door without waiting to say goodbye. It was only 9am on Sunday morning but I knew a pub in Acton that would have its back door open. This is where a lot of my mates went for the cure. After drinking there until about 12 noon, myself and another mate then got a taxi up to the Mean Fiddler in Harlesden where we knew there would be a live band playing until 3pm. That was the place to be on a Sunday for the craic back then.

After leaving the Fiddler shortly after 3pm, we somehow managed to lose each other in the crowd. My mate was also living in Acton, in a house that was also great for parties, so I decided I would make my way down there with the hope of meeting him again. Well we just seemed to both arrive at the same time despite taking different routes back. You would think we were long lost brothers who hadn't seen each other in years as we were both delighted to be reunited. There were two girls in the house so we asked them if they would like to join us for a drink. They accepted. So the four of us went to a pub of their choosing.

Everything was going good until the band started playing and myself and my mate got so high we started dancing on the tables and chairs. We were asked to leave and it was only then that we realised that our lady friends had disappeared. Standing outside the door considering our options, we both decided we would get a taxi and go to the National in Kilburn. It would have a band playing and we knew it stayed open late. We also figured that our two lady friends might also be there. But what we didn't think about was their strict dress code. My mate got stopped at the door by the bouncers as he was wearing runners. We were both so disappointed as we could hear the music blaring and we were also craving for more drink. As we walked down the street, feeling very sorry for ourselves, we noticed a wino sitting on the footpath wearing a pair of brown shoes that must have been at least a size 13. We approached him and, after explaining our situation, we asked him if he would he sell us his shoes. He said he would need £5 as well as my mate's runners to do a deal. But once we got his shoes on my mate's feet we ran off without honouring our side of the deal. The wino then gave us chase up Kilburn High Street in his bare feet shouting, 'Come back you thieving bastards.'

We did manage to gain entry into the National after that incident but not for very long. While we waited on our two pints my mate turned to me and said, 'Look at the size of my fucking two feet! I'll never get a woman in here tonight!' Our sides were sore from laughing at the size of the shoes and instead of just drinking our pints and behaving ourselves, we tipped the pints into each runner on the bar counter. We then continued by hitting our two empty glasses together, shouting cheers. But after that stunt we were both manhandled out the door by the bouncers, who had already been keeping a close eye on us. As well as my mate losing his runners which had cost him £70, we were both barred from future admission to the National. I suppose we got what we deserved for stealing the wino's shoes.

I never bothered going to work on Monday and, as I assumed I would probably be sacked anyway, I decided I would take the rest of the week off. On Thursday I went out to the job for my wages. Denis, my foreman, met me at the site gate and asked 'Where the fuck were you all week?' I told him I was away on the beer. Well, he told me that he had sacked men for missing just one day but he was prepared to give me a second chance. He then asked if I would come back in the morning and work Saturday and Sunday to make up my wages. Well, I did start back the next morning with good intentions of keeping straight, but on the Saturday evening after work, I went out on the town and ended up at another house party. I did go into work on Sunday morning but told Denis I was shattered and too hungover to stay on. Denis suggested that if I stayed on I could go for a cure at lunchtime. So I did. He joined me for a drink and when he told me he was from Glasgow, I told him that was a coincidence as my two friends, whose house I was partying in the previous night, were also from Glasgow. He told me to take the two boys out with me in the morning and he would give them a start on the job. Well I said, 'There's only one problem, Denis, they are both women!' He laughed at that and then asked if I was shagging them, I said, 'I wish I was.'

Three weeks later, I was still in the same job, when I received a letter notifying me of an appointment in Dublin for the following Tuesday morning. The appointment was with a psychiatrist, who was going to assess me on behalf of the insurance company. After another weekend of heavy drinking I didn't bother going to work. Once again I was just shattered and a bundle of nerves. I was now dreading my journey home, so I rang my doctor and arranged an appointment for later that same day. When he saw the state I was in, he wanted to admit me immediately to a detox unit. But I explained that I had to be in Dublin the following day and I needed something to calm my nerves. I told him about my previous experience, going into the horrors while travelling and that I was frightened it would happen to me again. Thankfully, he prescribed me some tablets, and he made me promise that once I returned to London I would seek help for my alcoholism.

After collecting my prescription, I took double my prescribed dosage and hoped for the best. I knew I had enough money for my return ticket. I figured it would be best to return the same day as I was in no form to spend a night in Dublin. I also decided that I would phone my mate, Leo, and get a sub off him as I wanted to be on the safe side. After meeting Leo and getting £300, I then went and booked my return flight. I now had £200 left and I was very tempted to go for a drink but decided I would go back to my room and wait and see if the tablets would make me feel any better.

Back in my room, I was sitting on the edge of the bed. I was soaking in my own sweat and the tablets still hadn't made me feel any better. My mate, Bob, then arrived at my bedroom door and I knew by looking at him that he was also suffering from the horrors. He asked me if I would come with him for a drink but I told him I was afraid to go drinking as I had to go to Dublin in the morning. I told him about my visit to the doctor and he then asked if I would give him a few tablets and he would just go home and go to bed. The mistake I made was to hand Bob the whole jar and I nearly passed out when he emptied out a handful and swallowed them. I was in bad enough shape myself before that happened but now I was feeling ten times worse. As well as getting robbed of most of my tablets, I was now worrying that Bob might have overdosed. As he was walking out the door he told me to phone him in the morning and he would come to Dublin with me for the craic. What made matters even worse was the fact that he was driving his own motorbike, a powerful 1000cc. The speed he took off up Horn Lane, I never thought he would make it home in one piece. But thank God he did.

Anyway after I counted what tablets I had left, I then took a few more. I lay down on top of my bed, dreading the night ahead. As well as feeling really frightened, I also felt so alone and wished I was at home with my family where I knew I would be safe. After tossing and turning and raving throughout the night I got up early in the morning to face the day ahead. By this stage I had no tablets left either so I said to myself, 'Fuck this, I need a drink.' I knew I didn't have too far to walk to my supplier so, after buying a bottle of whiskey, I booked a taxi for Heathrow to pick me up an hour later. I never bothered phoning Bob that morning and before my taxi arrived I was in such good form, I would have been happy to fly anywhere in the world. Somehow I managed to make it to Dublin that day for my appointment but my memory of it is next to none. The appointment with my psychiatrist must have passed off without incident. I'm sure he would have known that, as I was a chronic alcoholic, it was senseless even to try to have a conversation with me.

Chapter 20

On a Continuous Bender

After arriving back in London I didn't bother looking for any work, so for the next few months or so I just dossed about. But I was still drinking very heavily. When I moved into my digs first, I noticed there were housing benefit cheques coming in the post for names that I knew didn't live there. They had either been living there before I moved in, or else they didn't exist at all. What I did know however, was that whoever was lucky enough to get the post, could cash them for themselves. As I was the biggest dosser in the house I got most of them. I used to take them to a publican in East London who would charge £5 for cashing them. It was a good arrangement while it lasted. One day, after I had cashed one I continued drinking until closing time. I left the pub and waited for the last bus to Acton not realising I didn't keep the price of the fare home. I was afraid to risk walking home as I knew at least two other men who had been mugged around the same area. I now found myself stranded. Even though I didn't have any money to lose I certainly didn't want to get beaten up so I figured if I could find a safe place to lie down for the night, I would then walk home in the morning when it was clear.

As I was walking about looking, for my nest, I noticed a large flat roof. I figured this would be a safe place as I would be up off the ground and out of sight. There was a wall about four foot high going around the perimeter of it so, after climbing onto it, I then managed to get up onto the roof. I then noticed a TV aerial at the corner so after hanging my white shirt on it I then moved into the centre and lay down. I must have fallen into a sound sleep soon after that, because it was bright and clear when I awoke the following morning. It was a strange experience waking up that morning on a rooftop and one that I would not like to experience again. After putting my shirt back on, I had great difficulty getting back down on the ground as I was suffering from the shakes. Thankfully I managed it eventually without suffering any injuries. I then walked the journey back to Acton.

With Hughie Cullen at Newcastle Airport.

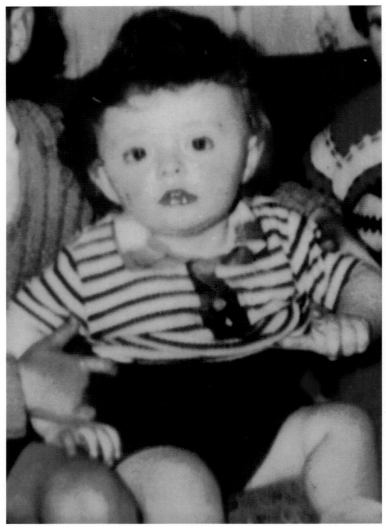

As a young baby

This photo was taken a few months before my accident in 1986, aged 23.
The scar on my right arm was as a result of one of my many scuffles.
The wound required 36 stitches.

With my much-loved Honda 70cc, aged 17

At the White House in 2000

At London City Airport with Gavin Smith and John McFadden.

With John McFadden in Galway in 1999

With my brother Edmund in 2005 at our home in Carrigart

My mother Sadie McFadden in 1997, the year before she died

My father James McFadden in 1992, the year before he died

As a young school boy

With my brother Edmund in 1993

My father's bicycle and turf spades fully restored and hanging proudly in my garage

With my beautiful wife Liz. For the record I was drinking water.

Myself and John McFadden

My father and mother James and Sadie McFadden

In Padua, Italy with the Basilica of St. Anthony in the background.

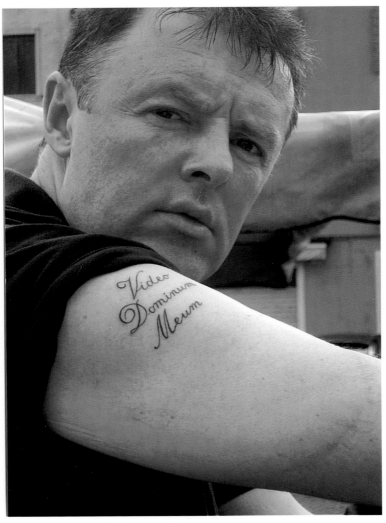

Showing off my tattoo which illustrates St. Anthony's final words,
'Video Dominum Meum' which translated means, 'I see my Lord.'
I had it done in Padua, Italy, home of St. Anthony's tomb.

I could remember everything about that particular episode, but one other morning shortly after that, I awoke in some woman's bed. I had no recollection whatsoever of meeting her so you can imagine my fright when I woke up in a strange bed with a strange woman. I hadn't a clue where I was and I was hoping I was still in London. To make matters worse I had managed to piss the bed for good measure. That woman did mention my mishap and said not to worry about it. She then suggested we move into to another room and into a dry bed. She was from London and owned the house we were in. Later that day I told her I wanted to pop out to a shop and buy a paper. I needed a drink, so my plan was to either get to an off licence or a pub – basically, whichever came first – and swallow over a few quick ones. I found myself beside a pub so, a few minutes later, I had four double vodkas inside me. After buying a paper, I was ready to go back to my friend's house. But what I didn't remember to do was to check the door number of the house or her address before I left. So I'm sad to say, I never did make it back to see my friend.

I did try and find her house but without success. I remembered the house had a white door and a cat sitting outside. So for the next half hour or so, I must have counted at least half a dozen white doors and ten different cats. It didn't matter how nice a date or how good a job opportunity was, I always managed to blow it. As long as I was drinking I would ruin my chances at everything.

I remember one other weekend I was out on a date. We were sitting in the beer garden. It was my lady friend's local bar. The place was really crowded when I noticed my brother, Edmund, making his way towards our table. It was a Sunday evening and he had stopped for a drink on his way home from his work. He was also a wild character and after shouting a loud 'Yahoo!' he then jumped up onto our table and said, 'Jesus, brother, I'm glad to see you.' He was still wearing his working boots, and needless to say, he spilled most of the drink and broke most of the glasses on the table. I didn't think there was much point introducing him properly to my date at that stage so when he said, 'Come on, brother and I'll buy you a drink.' I walked away from my friend and joined my brother at the bar. I knew now there wasn't much point in going back to my friend. She was really annoyed with my brother and, as well as that, I didn't have much money left but I knew Edmund would take care of that problem. I was also looking forward to a good old session as I knew drinks would be coming up fast and furious. It was also around this time that the three girls sharing our house moved out. They said they couldn't put up with our partying and wild ways any longer. Three fellows moved in shortly afterwards but they just kept to themselves. I knew they weren't impressed with our partying and that it would be only a matter of time before they reared up on us.

Once again, I got another letter stating that I was to go to Dublin for yet another appointment. It was now September and my solicitor said he hoped this would be the last time I would need to go. He said my case was listed for later that year and hopefully then it would be finalised. I was still living life on the edge. I got started on several jobs but again the usual thing would happen. I would mostly disappear before they had reason to sack me. I just didn't give a damn, as I wrongly believed back then that once I received my compensation I would change my way of living and make a new life for myself.

I approached Leo again for another sub of £200 and told him that when I received my compensation, I would pay him back. I now owed him £500. I was sober and in good form as I travelled to the Mater Private Hospital in Dublin for my check-up. This time I travelled by coach and boat as I had plenty of time. It was also less expensive. Arriving in Dublin early the next morning, I booked myself into a B&B near to the hospital where I had my appointment. I asked the landlady if I could have breakfast first and then get to bed for a few hours. She said it was no problem and just charged me £10 punts. After my check-up, which I thought went quite well, I decided I would have a drink. I met two girls at the bar in the bus depot who were on their way to a party in Navan, Co. Meath. After a good few drinks, I was very tempted to go with them. The only reason I didn't was because I knew I wouldn't have enough money for the fare to London the following day. I'm not sure if they ever did get to Navan that night because they had already missed the bus that they had intended taking. After exchanging details, they promised they would visit me and they wished me luck as I left for my overnight return trip back to London.

When I arrived back at my house, I had my disability benefit and two of my anonymous friends' housing benefit cheques to cash. So later that day I met up with my mate, Noel. I hadn't seen him since the day we took the rocking chair. The next morning we both awoke after spending the night on a floor. We were in a flat in Hammersmith. There was a bottle of whiskey and a bottle of vodka beside us. I was shivering with the cold and my body was all aches and pains. I asked the woman, whom I assumed owned the flat, to put the kettle on as I was looking forward to having a hot whiskey. She then informed me that was not possible as we were in a squat that had its electricity disconnected. After drinking our bottles straight, the three of us then went drinking around a few different bars in the area. That night we ended up in the Archway Tavern on Holloway Road. Everything was going good until it was time to leave. We got into our taxi and Noel jumped in the front while myself and our lady friend got in the back. Another man, whom I had not seen before, then gets into our taxi. I was in great form so I attempted to sing a song. I knew I was not a very good singer but when our "unknown" passenger told me to shut my mouth up, I took offence and asked him if he was looking for a fight. When he said that he was, the taxi driver stopped abruptly and told us all to get out. Myself and my fighting partner started exchanging punches and by now were out in the middle of a busy street. I was coming under pressure so my mate, Noel, came to my rescue and hit my opponent a powerful uppercut which knocked him to the ground. Noel then put his big arm around my shoulder and said, 'We had to go for a knockout.'

By now the police had arrived on the scene and, after arresting us, they then brought us to a police station and locked us up in separate cells for the night. We were lucky as we never got charged for that incident. The next day we got released at different times. When it was my turn to get out I asked the policeman where I was. He informed me that we were in King's Cross. I then made my way back to dear old Acton alone.

After that I continued dossing for quite a while and continued surviving on my benefits. I was still going on wild benders. Even sometimes if I had the good intentions of getting back on track, someone would just arrive with a carry out and it could be days, or sometimes weeks, before you might get sober again. It worked both ways, as numerous times I would just turn up at a mate's door when I wanted someone to join me for a session. I also found myself barred from several pubs again. One bar in particular, I thought I had been barred unfairly from. I was in the company of two men who started fighting with each other, but I was also asked to leave, which I did. I figured everything would be ok for the next time I went back as I wasn't fighting.

The following morning I arrived in on my own but the landlord soon informed me that I was barred. I was surprised and asked him what I was barred for as I hadn't done anything. He simply replied by saying, 'I can bar whoever I want.' I walked out and went into the next pub as I needed a drink. My form was too bad to argue or let him know I was not very happy with his decision. I continued drinking that day and night and figured that, if I was already barred for nothing, I might as well give him a good reason to bar me for good.

When I arrived in again, the bar was packed. As I made my way towards the counter the landlord produced a baton and said, 'I think it is time you were leaving.' I replied back by saying, 'Maybe it's time you were leaving yourself.' I then fired a large jug of water over the counter. It just missed him but it made pieces of a very large mirror. In the space of about another 30 seconds I had smashed two windows and had also pulled a large chandelier from the ceiling, which landed on top of a group of men who were playing cards. I managed to escape just in time as the landlord and a group of angry card players were coming at me. As I ran I knew I had to get off the streets. I also wanted more drink. After passing a small hotel, I then booked myself a room and continued drinking alone in the bar. As I listened to the police sirens outside I wondered if they were looking for me.

Chapter 21

Working in a Brewery

After arriving in one Monday morning to my local Windmill pub, the landlady told me there was a job going in the brewery. She said she knew the boss very well and if I was interested she would put in a good word for me. I said I was very interested and promised her I wouldn't mess things up if I got the job. She rang the boss and gave me a good reference over the phone. I was then informed that I could start the following morning. I was delighted and was now looking forward to my new job. It was about six weeks before Christmas. I reported, bright and early, for work the following morning and my first job was to help to load the lorry. When we were finished I was told that I would be helping with the deliveries around the various bars and clubs in London. I was also informed that I would be paid cash which suited me just fine.

The driver was from London and, as we set off on our first delivery, he explained that every pub we delivered to would put up a drink or two afterwards. As he couldn't drink and drive he would just take the price of the drinks instead. It was a pity that I didn't choose the same sensible option but being an alcoholic I thought I was on to a great number. The first week went well and I was really happy in my new job. I had also got reinstated in one bar that I had been previously barred from. I couldn't believe it when, on my second day, we stopped outside it. I explained to the driver my situation and he said he knew the Governor. The reason I got barred the last time I had been in, was because I had brought a bottle of gin in with me and ended up dancing on the table. I didn't even like gin but I had lifted it as I was leaving a party earlier that same day and thought that I had might as well drink it.

Things were looking good once again. On Sunday morning I decided I would go down to the Windmill for a drink as I had the day off. During the course of the day I got talking to a fellow I had never met before, so I included him in my round and bought him a pint (for the purposes of this story we shall refer to him as Matt, I didn't get his name). It was normal on a Sunday to get into rounds. So on that particular day there was a large group of men in the same company so every time someone bought a round they included Matt as they had assumed he was a mate of mine. After being bought a large amount of drink, Matt then asked me for a sub of £10. He explained that he had just come in for a few quiet pints and hadn't been prepared for joining company and buying rounds. Once he got his £10 from me, he said he would buy his round and square me up again. He also asked to keep our transaction a secret. After I passed him the £10 he still made no attempt to buy a drink. Then one of the lads in our company asked me, 'What kind of a bollocks is that you're with?' I told him I didn't know him and had only met him for the first time that morning.

As well as not buying a drink, Matt started slagging off our county football team. I knew then that I was going to confront him but as I didn't want to cause any trouble, out of my respect for the landlady, I suggested to Matt that we would go next door to the Blarney Stone for a pint. I also decided I would take my drink with me so as to make sure that Matt would have to buy. As we both made our way next door we never spoke and, once inside, I walked over to a table and sat down with my precious drink (a double brandy). When Matt joined me, empty handed, I couldn't help but say, 'Is it not time you were buying a drink?' Jesus, he then flew into a rage and pulled a bundle of money from his pocket and said, 'I could buy a fucking drink if I wanted to.' He was now towering over me, so once I apologised and got him settled and seated, I hit him a thump which knocked him off his chair and across the floor. I assumed I would be barred, so I swallowed my drink and walked out. Back in the Windmill, I discovered my friend, Matt, had got £10 from at least six other men in my company. What I also discovered was that I didn't get barred from the Blarney Stone. When I did venture in again I apologised to the landlord. He then said to me, 'I'm sorry as well that you didn't hit that cunt half hard enough.'

I remember we were doing a delivery to a club in the city one particular day. The driver informed me it was a gay bar. Once we got the required order delivered via the cellar, the driver then spoke into an intercom on the door allowing us to gain entry. I was enjoying my pint inside when I started to quiz the woman behind the bar about 'What people really got up to in here?' She asked me why I wanted to know. I said my heart was broken trying to find a woman and that I might consider all options. She was now staring me straight in the eye to see if I was serious. When I was in good form I never had a problem putting on a good act. She then produced an application form for me to fill in, which I did, but I gave my roommate's name instead. I was now looking forward to seeing his expression when his membership card arrived in the post.

About one week before Christmas, I was in a bar after work having a drink. I met a girl who was going to be in London for a few days so I hooked up with her and I never bothered going into work the following morning. As much as I enjoyed my work I just couldn't leave my friend, as I promised her I would keep her company for the next few days and show her some of the sights of London. That was the end of my career with the brewery.

Chapter 22

Going Home for Christmas

I did manage to make it home for Christmas. I got a lift with a mate who was taking his car. I didn't have much money but it didn't matter as once I got home I knew I would be ok. That was the beauty of being at home. You always had a nice warm bed, plenty of food in the fridge, and if you had any beer money that was an added bonus. I was an awful worry on my parents and so I knew any time we spent together was precious. My father often said to me that he wished I would meet a good woman and settle down as he wouldn't be around forever. My father was over 50 years of age when I was born. He was a smart man and he knew that time was not on his side now. I never wanted to hurt him but as long as I continued drinking, I was going to be in trouble and getting myself into all sorts of crazy situations.

My mate, Noel, also made it home that Christmas and, somehow, we both managed to land in a nightclub which was 35 miles from our home. The next morning I woke up in someone's coal shed. I was sitting in an armchair which had its cushion removed and I could feel the springs cutting into my arse. I looked across and could see Noel fast asleep on the floor. He was using a bag of coal as a pillow. When I woke him I could not help but laugh, as his face was all black from the coal. We left the coal shed and began to make our way home on foot. I figured it must have been very early as the whole town seemed deserted. None of us had a watch. The next thing, I noticed a woman walking on the other side of the road so I called out to her to give us the time. She must have thought we had been dropped from a spaceship because she took off running like hell. We were both freezing with the cold and in bad need of a drink, not to mention a good shower, when a bus pulls in at a bus stop. I race over and hop on first. I asked the driver where we were heading to and he replied, 'Derry.' So I said, 'That sounds good to me.'

Noel sat down next to me and asked where this bus was going. I told him it was going to Letterkenny. You see, Noel was anxious to get home to Carrigart but I didn't care. I was happy as long as I had a seat and was in out of the cold. When Noel finally realised the route the bus was taking, he shouted at the driver to put his foot on the brake. He then says to me, 'Do you not think it was bad enough landing me in Ballybofey last night without now trying to take me to Derry?' We got off the bus and started walking towards Letterkenny. After walking for about an hour, we finally got a lift into Letterkenny where we got the cure. We then hitched a lift to Carrigart and went our separate ways.

I didn't bother going out for the remainder of the festive season. Edmund was also home from London. He was coping much better than I was in the 'Big Smoke' and had been in the same job in Newbury since the summer. He told me he would get me the start on it once we got back in the New Year.

On my way back to London I was in great form and looking forward to the year ahead. My solicitor said that all was going well with my case and it would be finalised within the next three months or so. Things were looking good for me once again. I now thought I had everything figured out. I would go to work with Edmund, ease up on my drinking and, once I received my compensation, I would come back home and settle down.

Chapter 23

Working in Newbury

Little did I know that on my first day in Newbury, this was going to be my last job in England. We got picked up outside the office in Shepherds Bush each morning. Several vans would then travel out together as there were a large body of men employed. It was good fun coming home each evening as the drivers would all race each other. However, they never seemed to be in the same panic in the morning.

Leo, our boss, said that never again would he allow so many alcoholics and so many head cases on the same job. I had suggested to Leo that he should keep some money out of my wages each week as I wanted to repay my debt. But he never did. Edmund took me under his wing and on my first day he introduced me to all the lads on the job as the 'wee brother'. I was then told I would be working alongside Edmund. If I had been paired off with a stranger I would not have survived my first day. Edmund was well at himself at the time so he took care of any heavy lifting or anything that was a bit tricky for me. I remember thinking to myself that same day that I was in 'quare' bad shape. I knew that if I could get the first week over and stay sober that I would get broken in again and become more able and fitter. I also had the good intentions of keeping my New Year resolutions, but they went out the window once I got my first pay packet.

I was now back at my binge drinking and disappearing acts. Jack, our ganger man was one great boss. One day on the job, after I had consumed one too many, Jack called me aside and says, 'Follow me young man. I'm not going to sack you. I just want to show you a place where you can sleep it off.' One other day, after I arrived back from the pub, Jack asked me if I had seen Jonathan and Maurice who had also gone missing. Jack was in a bit of a panic and says, 'The fucking agent is after landing on the job.' I said that I would go and get them and so off I went back to the pub. They were just finishing their pints and preparing to leave when I entered. Maurice asked me if anyone had missed them off the job. I said, 'I don't think so,' and ordered us three double brandies. That evening at the end of the shift, the van driver arrived at the pub and found the three of us full of brandy trying to sing The Fields of Athenry. I never bothered going into work the following morning and instead went off on anther serious bender which landed me in Luton. I did go back out to work again a few days later, as Jack was asking for me and said everything would be ok if I returned to work.

Back in my digs we had new house mates. As well as our wild partying, the house itself had deteriorated was in bad need of some decor. Myself and my mate were still sharing the same room and we now discovered another great form of amusement. One day we were watching as a new pay phone was being erected on the other side of the street, exactly opposite our house. After taking a note of its number, we would then sit at our window and wait for people to walk by before dialling it. As our ground floor was occupied by a 24 hour mini-cab office we were never short of customers.

We had a good relationship with the drivers and we never gave them any bother. I remember one day the owner of the mini-cab office telling me that in the ten years he had been there, the house parties just got crazier after we moved in. He also said that I was fucking crazy also. But he agreed that we were 'good for business'. One other day, after I had booked a taxi, I invited the driver to join me for a drink. He took me up on my offer and we embarked on a pub crawl around the various bars in London. My good friend from Pakistan was not too worried about drinking and driving and that night we ended up in a nightclub in Southall where he figured we would both score with the opposite sex. However, the only thing we scored that night was the side of his taxi, after he fell asleep driving us home and crashed into another car. I was sorry later when I heard that he lost his job because of that incident. I knew only too well what it was like to get sacked.

Chapter 24

Starting in Newbury for a Second Time

I went away on another bender, but did start back again in Newbury, as I had promised Edmund I would give it another go. There was always great banter among the lads on that job as there were so many characters together. My brother Edmund was a real character himself. One day he asked Jack, our ganger man, for a kango hammer. The building we were working on was an extension to a Marks and Spencer store, which was still open for business. When Jack asked Edmund what he needed a kango for, Edmund then points towards a window in the clothes department, which has a large female dummy inside. Edmund then declares, 'It's been a long time since I got a ride, so give me that kango and I will cut a fucking hole in that dummy in there.'

There were a lot of funny moments like that on that job. But the amount of drink that was consumed was unreal. I said to Edmund one day that I was jacking the work in, as I figured it was costing me more to come to work. I was also a danger to myself and anyone else who was near me. One day, when I was both drunk and in the horrors, I fell down a hole in the roof that had been left to erect a lift shaft in. What made that accident more amazing was the fact that I had earlier been given the responsibility of making it safe. I fell twelve feet onto hard concrete and landed on my back. I landed beside a fellow who got such a fright that he just ran away without waiting to attend to me. I spent the next three weeks on crutches, but it didn't stop me from drinking or from getting myself into trouble. The boys on the job did a collection and the following evening Edmund called up to my house with the kitty.

Things in the house started going from bad to worse. We had nothing in common with our new house mates. We did try to make them feel welcome but they just seemed to keep themselves to themselves. I suppose in order to enjoy my company, you would have to be both alcoholic and a crazy man.

One night Stephen, our new housemate, was trying to wind myself and my room mate up and he succeeded. So we decided we would pay him a visit. But our plan was misguided as he had retreated to his bedroom and locked his door. I suppose anyone else in our position would consider one of the two obvious options – either burst the door in or leave it until he decided to come out again. Well we just had to be different. His room was next to ours so we knew that the bed he slept in was parallel to mine. We then started to knock a hole through the wall. We didn't have the proper tools for such a job and just used a small hammer and a small piece of iron. By the time we did get through to the other side our friend was long gone. We didn't hear him leave the previous night as we were both too busy hammering and laughing.

I remember the next day trying to cover the hole over my bed with a large poster. We did try to cover up Stephen's side of the wall with a large painting that had been hanging in our hall. There were so many crazy incidents in that house that I'm sure that if some of its former tenants got together and shared their memories, there would be no problem filling a few more chapters.

There were also a lot of tragedies attached to that same house. Quite a large number of young men who had either lived, or partied there, have since died. I did wonder sometimes if there was some sort of curse attached to it. It was also around this time that I lost my two anonymous friends' social security cheques that I had been cashing. One morning at 9am I answered the phone to some gentleman who had said he wanted to speak with a Mr. So & So. I was caught unawares and told him he didn't live there anymore. It was when he asked who he was speaking to, that I became suspicious and hung up the phone. When the phone rang the following morning at the same time, I recognised his voice. This time he said he was looking for a Miss So & So who he said was an old college friend. I told him I would check her room to see if she was in. Later that same day, two officers from the local Social Security office visited our house to carry out investigations on housing benefit claims.

Our local pub also got a new landlord and he said that he wouldn't tolerate any messing so we all knew it was only a matter of time before we got barred. One Monday, I remember there were thirteen of us in the same company, so as you can imagine there was loud banter and good craic. We had been issued with several warnings to quieten down but it just fell on deaf ears. My brother Edmund then decided to jump up on the pool table where he starts dancing and singing and using the cue stick as a microphone. The landlord approached me and asked me to get my brother down off the table, so I said, 'No problem.' I then got hold of the other cue stick and smashed the lights above the pool table while telling Edmund to get down before he would break something. I know it was crazy and reckless but that was how we were living our lives back then.

I did venture in again one day when I was on my own. The bar woman informed me that I was barred and if I wanted to plead my case I would have to speak with the landlord. So she explained that he was having a shower and would be down shortly. Without a second thought, I raced up the stairs and confronted him in the bathroom. He was trying to shave but I knocked him to the floor. I suppose I should mention that he was also completely naked. He told me to settle down and to go down to the bar and have a drink and he would join me later. As I was leaving the bathroom, I noticed the electric razor on the bathroom floor buzzing away. He had dropped it during the melee. I did get three double brandies in me before the police arrived and arrested me.

I would just like to add, for the record, that I have since met this landlord and apologised for that incident. I met him during one of my weekends back in London in a nightclub. I shook his hand and we had a laugh and a good drink that same night. It was nice to meet him as a person and not in his role as a landlord.

Chapter 25

Third and Final Time in Newbury

Once again Edmund asked me to start back at work in Newbury. The job was near completion. I thought it would be nice to see some of the lads again so on my first day back Jack showed me a large flat roof. He told me it had to be painted and I would be working with a fellow from Greece. I had been hoping he would send me with some of my mates who I could have the craic with. I tried talking to the Greek but he couldn't understand a word I was saying. I thought to myself, "fuck this, I'm not going to spend a few days up here with you." It was also the same roof I had earlier fallen through, so my heart was not too bothered about doing a good job. I noticed a large sweeping brush so I got myself a plan. The paint was stacked in five gallon containers. I started emptying the paint onto the roof in different places. I then got hold of the sweeping brush and started levelling it out. I was working at a furious rate. The Greek approached me with his hands flying in the air, indicating for me to stop. But I ignored him and reached for another container of paint. He was now standing in front of me in protest. I told him to get the fuck out of my way. When he ignored me I emptied some paint over his feet. That changed his mind and as he tried to run away from me I followed him throwing out large puddles of paint.

Two agents then arrived up beside us on the roof. I was busy with my sweeping and they just stared at me in disbelief. As well as painting the Greek's shoes, I had also covered tiles, timbers and part of a skylight. One of the agents then remarked that I was doing a fine job so I thought one sarcastic remark deserved another! I replied by saying, 'My brush is a bit on the small side.' I then fired my brush into a skip that was sitting on the ground below. That was my last job in England.

It was also around this time that I got called in front of the Disability Board and summoned to see a doctor. The appointment was in Ealing and I knew if

I walked the whole way there, my feet would be swollen, so that's what I did. After examining me and hearing my very sad story, the doctor gave me the taxi fare home out of his own pocket. I also received a pension book and I thought I was elected.

My social life in Acton was now becoming much similar to that of home. I found myself barred from a lot of bars. One day I was drinking in one of my locals when a gypsy women entered. But not long after she was told she was barred and was asked to leave. I called her over and invited her to join me for a drink. When I had money on me I made sure I always had a good supply in front of me. I got into this habit of ordering four drinks at a time for myself and if it was last orders I could ask for any amount. Well anyway, the gypsy woman took me up on my offer and after drinking all my drink she then grabbed me by the hair and pulled me off my stool. I landed on my back halfway across the floor. When I got back on my feet again my mate, Noel, was dancing around the pool table with her. I couldn't help but laugh and needless to say I was after losing another pub.

One other night, after another session, I went into a Kentucky Fried Chicken outlet. There were three men standing at the counter and after placing my order one of them accused me of jumping the queue. I knew I didn't but I decided to apologise as I knew they were looking for trouble. Once I apologised I knew it was a waste of time as they were still on my case. After turning and pretending to walk away, I suddenly made a 180 degree turn and hit the mouth that was doing most of the talking. Once outside I tried to make my escape, when one of them clobbered me over my head with a plank of timber. It knocked me straight to the ground and, only the police arrived at the same time, I know I would have been seriously injured. That particular wound to my head required seven stitches. The police arrested the fellow who clobbered me but I signed a form saying I wasn't going to press any charges. I didn't want the hassle and, anyway, I figured it wouldn't speed up the healing process for my head.

Chapter 26

My £90,000 Compensation

My solicitor rang me and informed me that the insurance company had made us an offer of £90,000 punts. They would also pay all legal costs, as well as my hospital bills, which amounted to £24,000. It was their third and final offer. We could go into court but there was no guarantee we would get any more. There was also the danger of getting less. As I wasn't in permanent employment before my accident I couldn't claim loss of earnings. It was also pointed out to me that I was already lying on the ground when I was run over and had a high amount of alcohol consumed, meaning that I was partly to blame. We accepted their offer and on my birthday, 3rd May, 1990, I received my cheque for £90,000. I was 27 years old. As it would take a few days for the cheque to clear, I borrowed £200 from a mate as I wanted to celebrate and have a good drink for my birthday. After paying off any debts I had at home, and dividing out £5,000 between my family members, I once again headed back to London. I also had some debt to settle there and was anxious to get that out of the way.

When I went down to the office, Leo advised me to go back to work. All I wanted that morning was to square up my debt. Being an alcoholic and craving for drink, you must understand that going back to work was the last thing on my mind. Later that day, in a pub in Acton, I met two sisters. I told them I was just after arriving in London. What I 'forgot' to mention was the fact that I had already been living there before and would have been known in a lot of bars in Acton and barred from quite a few of them. Every time it was my round I would buy four vodkas for myself and doubles for the girls. After quite a few rounds, the girls suggested that we go back to their house for something to eat, otherwise we would never stick the pace. One of them also said she would like me to meet her husband, who was also a bit of a character. After having a nice meal and too much wine back in the house, the girls then suggested that the four of us would go down to their local for a drink. They said I would meet a lot of Donegal folk there. Jesus, I now was in a bit of a predicament. I was already barred but decided I would say nothing and go with the flow. As we entered the bar I made sure I was last in and I was probably hoping that there might be someone new behind the bar who would not know me. Well, I wasn't that lucky and the next thing I see is the landlord raising his hands in the air and shouting, 'Get him out of here!' Well the girl who had told me I would get on well with her 'bit of a character' husband was spot on, because the next thing I know he attacks the landlord and knocks him to the ground. He then turns to me saying, 'That fucker must be off his head, as you're only off the boat.'

That night we all went next door to another bar and had a good laugh. The landlord there must have been a character also because he seemed to be able to handle things when they got out of hand. I remember one night myself and my brother Edmund fighting with some other customers and they never bothered barring us. He was probably one of the smarter ones, as the amount of drink we were consuming was beyond belief, so it was well worth it for him financially to put up with a bit of banter and maybe the odd racket. Anyone who showed us respect, we would show them respect in return.

Before my accident I would have been notorious for fighting in bars and nightclubs and quite rightly got barred. But what used to really annoy and anger me was when I got barred for my reputation and not my actions. When that happened I would almost certainly return and start wrecking the place. Even though I am sober writing this and well settled, it's something I can't say that I'm sorry about. When you take on the responsibility of a pub, I think you can expect the unexpected. Most of the landlords are just ruthless and shrewd business people. However, some of them are genuine and caring people.

Chapter 27

On Another Continuous Bender

I was now on a continuous bender in London and I'm now certain that, only I had St. Anthony watching over me, I would never have survived those years. One morning, after drinking a bottle of vodka in my digs, I decided I was going home. I never bothered packing a bag and a few hours later I was having a drink in Dublin. I phoned home and was talking to my father who said he was glad I was on my way home. He said we would go to the bog together the following morning. I don't know what came over me but later that same day I was on another flight back to London.

That night I went for a drink with a girl I had just met. She had no idea the amount of alcohol I had consumed and when I told her that I had been in Dublin earlier that day for a drink she didn't believe me. She suggested we go to the Elephant and Castle pub. She ordered a half pint of lager so I thought I would take it easy myself and I ordered a pint. I was struggling with my pint but Angie had her glass empty in record time so we ordered the same again. As Angie was now making short work of her second drink, I knew I was under pressure so I went back up to the bar again. This time I ordered four half pints of lager and four vodkas and coke. When I arrived back down at our table with my packed tray of drink, Angie looked flabbergasted and was embarrassed, explaining that everybody in the pub knew her. A few minutes later, I had swallowed my four shorts and went to the bar again and ordered four more. I was on a real high and I was sore from laughing as the drinks were stocking up in front of Angie. After that my memory is blank, but I was told we did make it to a karaoke night in another bar up the street. The next day I met Angie again for a drink in a pub in Ealing. Everything went normal for the first few hours but later that day I pulled the same stunt. I started ordering drinks again in batches of four.

There were some days when I would drink three bottles of vodka or brandy and still remember everything. I also had the habit of changing my drinks. Sometimes I would do binges on brandy, vodka or whiskey. If I was in real bad form I would start the day drinking brandy or port or, if I was feeling cold, I would start drinking hot whiskey. It was around this time that I decided to move out of Horn Lane. I knew if I was to have any chance of getting sorted out I would have to make a move. Our digs was one wild house back then. We had the Christmas decorations up during the summer and it was also possible for anything to go flying out the windows. When we'd finish drinking a bottle of vodka or brandy or whatever, it was not unusual to see the empty bottle flying out the window. Somebody once threw the television out and, one other night, one of the lads jumped out and broke his ankle in the process. We also used to put cans of body spray or something similar on top of the gas cooker. When it exploded it would make an awful bang.

One day, I remember one of the sensible, or maybe normal, lodgers had several pots on, cooking dinner. He must have been expecting female company because he had the table nicely set. When I got him out of the kitchen, I placed a large tin of hair moose on the cooker. When it exploded there was white foam all over the kitchen. Needless to say, the cook wasn't very popular with the rest of the housemates and when he complained, one of the lads said it would go well with the Christmas decorations.

Shortly after that I moved out of Horn Lane and moved into a house in Kensington. It was a well maintained house. I continued on my bender and never bothered looking for work. The first day I moved in I rang my sister with my new address and phone number. Later that same day when I was out checking out the tubes and buses, I realised I had not kept a copy of the address myself. I couldn't remember it so I had to phone my sister back and ask her where I was living. After that I made sure I wrote it down.

Chapter 28

Meeting Karen

One week later, myself and a mate called Paul were walking up Churchfield Road in Acton. It was about 8pm in the evening. We were both well steamed. I noticed a girl walking down the other side of the street so I called over and asked if she would like to join us for a drink. She was wearing ear phones so she crossed over to our side. As she removed her ear phones, Paul took a back step as he was certain she was going to thump me one. I asked her again if she would like to join me for a drink and, to our surprise, she replied, 'Sure, let's go.' The three of us then went to the first pub that I wasn't barred from. The drinks were coming up fast and furious and I was putting them away just as the barman was handing them to me. Needless to say, I soon forgot about my date but my mate, Paul, didn't and he later walked her home.

The next morning I awoke, and figuring Paul would not be at work, I called up to his house. I wanted a good mate to go on the session with. When I got into the house Paul was already on the phone to his new woman. She told Paul she would meet him at 1pm, in exactly the same place where I had called her over. She told Paul to bring me with him as she had a real nice friend for me. Paul was all business but all I wanted that morning was more drink. After getting the cure we made our way to the arranged location, and sure enough, the two girls were waiting for us. After getting introduced to Karen I thought I wouldn't have a hope in hell of shifting her. I really fancied her and thought to myself that she could have any man she wanted. But I decided I would chance my arm and ask her out. I thought, she will refuse and then I'll be free to go back to the pub and have a good drink! But when Karen said yes, I was both surprised and delighted.

Karen was from the North East of England, Newcastle to be precise. She had moved down to London and was now living as a live-in childminder. She had to be back in her house by 10pm each weekday night but had her weekends free. Our first week went great. We met every day at lunchtime and we would go to the park with the two children she was taking care off. Karen was free each evening after 6pm so we would meet again and spend four hours together before she had to go home. The first weekend we were together I took her on a tour of the bars and clubs. The following Tuesday lunchtime I told Karen that I had to go and meet with a man who was giving me a job. But Karen was not going to be fooled so easy, and she told me she knew I was just going to the pub. So, with that, I invited her to join me. She said she couldn't as she had the two children with her, but I told her it wouldn't be a problem as I knew a pub where we could go for a few quiet drinks where nobody would bother us. We were still there at 6pm when Karen was due to finish for the evening. So we ordered a taxi to take us all back to Karen's place. At that time I would have thought it was normal to go drinking during the day and wouldn't have realised how serious it was to bring Karen and the two children into the bar with me.

I waited for Karen in the taxi as she took the children inside. Once she had that sorted I figured we could go and enjoy a good drink. It wasn't long until I heard the shouting and the next thing I know, Karen's belongings are flying out onto the street in black bin-liners. I asked the taxi driver to wait for me so that I could go and see if Karen was ok. When Karen's boss saw me walking up his footpath, he screamed at me to 'Get the fuck of his property,' and that he was going to call the police. Once I realised Karen was safe, I gathered up her belongings and put them in our taxi. It was a bad situation. As well as Karen losing her job, she now had no place to stay, so I asked her if she wanted to move in with me until she got herself sorted. I felt guilty and knew it was all my fault. So a week after our first meeting, we now found ourselves living together. I still hadn't told Karen about getting my compensation so every day she would suggest that we'd both look for work, as we couldn't continue drinking and dossing about. She also said that once we were both working we would then get ourselves a flat.

Karen did apply for several jobs but I just couldn't get motivated or sober. One morning, I decided on the spur of the moment, as usual, that I would move home. I thought I would have a better chance of getting off the drink and getting my life sorted out. When I told Karen my plan she then asked, 'And what about me?' I said she was more than welcome to come with me. That night Karen and myself landed in my home in dear old Carrigart.

The house itself at that time was very basic, to say the least. We still didn't have a bathroom, no running hot water, and our toilet was located in an out-house, that was known as our coalhouse. So it meant getting up and going out in the middle of the night if nature called. Our heating system consisted of an old range in the kitchen, which was also used for cooking. There were two open fireplaces, in what was, a very small sitting room and a fairly large bedroom. It was pointless trying to put a fire on in either. They were both so small that if the wind was blowing the wrong way, you would need an oxygen mask to stay in the place. Anyway it was the house where I was born and the one place on earth where I felt safe and secure and greatly loved.

After introducing Karen to my father, I suggested we would need another bed. My father then asked me how many beds we used in London and when I answered just the one, he replied, 'Well, sure the one will be enough for you here as well and there's no need to be putting extra expense on yourselves.' Although my father was well on in years, he was smart and broad-minded. As long as I was safe and happy he was pleased for us. He was delighted to have us home. Karen and myself did try to settle down, but Carrigart must have seemed a lot different from her home in Newcastle. We still didn't have a telephone installed in our house and it was three days later when Karen eventually got to phone home to tell her mother where she was.

We didn't have a television either, so one day we went to Letterkenny and I ended up buying a 14 inch portable television, the cheapest one in the shop! Was that not crazy or what? I then hired a contractor to do some work on our home. Nothing fancy but just the basics. We needed a bathroom, new doors and windows, and we really needed oil fired central heating installed. The contractor quoted me a price of £15,000 which I thought was good. He explained he was very busy at that particular time but would get back to me at a later date.

Chapter 29

Living with Karen

As good as my intentions were to get some sort of routine back in my life, I just couldn't keep away from the drink. There was no such thing as staying at home for a night, watching our 14 inch TV or just having an early night. My whole life at that time revolved around alcohol and I never gave any other sort of entertainment a second thought. Here I was, with a gorgeous girlfriend who I was crazy about. Anyone who knew me at that time must have thought I had it all. I had Karen, who stood by me no matter what scrapes I got into, and I still had most of my compensation. I wasn't in receipt of any benefits at that time. Looking at the bigger picture I was on the road to destruction. I was unemployed and an alcoholic. I was so unsettled and unpredictable. I could have decided on the spur of the moment to just take off again and to anywhere.

Karen seemed happy with our situation for a while. I always remember her singing and laughing around our house as she kept herself busy washing and scrubbing our house from top to bottom. Karen also came with us when we went to the bog to bring the turf home and she could carry the bags as well as any man. As I didn't have a car we had to depend on other people's generosity to bring us to town or to the pubs. But often we would just head off walking.

As you can imagine it wasn't long until we both got bored. I was still barred from most of the surrounding bars and nightclubs so, once again, we decided to go back to London and promised ourselves we would get a nice place to stay and get jobs. I suppose the next mistake I made was going back and getting a room for us in a large house in Acton. I was almost as well known in parts of Acton then as I was at home, so my chances of getting my life in order there were not good. Karen did make a few serious attempts to find a job but she was too busy trying to watch me and keep me out of trouble. The amount of drink I was consuming was serious and when I wasn't stoned out of my head, I was suffering from the horrors and hearing all sorts of crazy things in my head. I was lucky I had Karen by my side then as she was always watching out for me. At that time I was so paranoid and shaken that she would have to take me by the hand and help me across the street. One day I decided we would go up to North London. I had a few mates living there whom I hadn't seen for some time. Myself and Karen met up with them in a bar on Holloway Road, so needless to say we all had a good session.

After agreeing a price with a mini cab driver, myself and Karen set off on our journey back to Acton. As we were approaching Harlesden I noticed the metre had already reached the fare we had agreed on, so I confronted the driver and asked what the fuck he was playing at. When I told him he wasn't getting a penny more than the price we had agreed, he stopped the taxi suddenly, got out of the car and opened the boot. I thought to myself that he must have a weapon in there, so I decide to throw myself at him and I threw a few punches. We were fighting in the middle of the street and we were disrupting the traffic, and all I could hear were horns blowing and people shouting at us. It was at this stage that Karen came to my rescue. She attacked the driver with a length of timber she had managed to get her hands on. He must have figured then that he wasn't going to beat us both, so he made a run for it and hopped back into the car.

Well, we still needed a lift so I managed to get back in beside him and I held the handbrake until Karen got on board. He then shouted at me, 'Do you want to get out or go to Acton Police Station?' But before I got the chance to reply, Karen told him to take us to the police station if he wanted. Jesus, I didn't want to go into a police station but Karen said, 'Don't worry, honey, everything will be alright.' Sure enough the driver landed us at the station and he made a complaint against us for assault. Karen explained to the policeman that the driver had attempted to grope her and that I had stepped in to save her. When she was asked to make a statement, she said she would accept an apology if the driver withdrew his complaint against me. Needless to say, that was the last we heard of that incident.

Well, I continued on my bender and over the next few months myself and Karen landed back in Donegal. Once again, I was heading to the security of my home but I couldn't get sober long enough to face reality. One time, we left my house in Carrigart to go to Karen's home in Newcastle. The obvious route to take was to go to Belfast and then get a direct flight to Newcastle, but nothing was straightforward with me when I was drinking. I somehow managed to land us both in Dublin first and then Glasgow before eventually reaching Newcastle about one week later. After staying at Karen's home for some time, we both decided we would move back to London and make another attempt at it.

Once again I got us another room in Acton. This time the house we moved into was situated beside the A40 motorway. I still don't know how many rooms were let in that house, but for the duration of our stay there, we never met any other lodgers. I do remember phoning the landlord several times asking him to collect his rent from me because, deep down, I probably knew I would just get up and take off again out of the blue.

Chapter 30

A Rocky Relationship

Karen did leave me. She had been pleading with me to ease up on the drink. She didn't have a problem with me having a drink and was not asking me to stop completely, but she said that if I continued on drinking like I was, then I was either going to kill myself or end up in prison. She did say that if I got myself sorted I could call her in a few weeks time at home in Newcastle. She was missing home a lot, which was only natural, as Karen was only 22 years old at that time.

With Karen gone I continued on my binges. In the mornings I would go to the off licence and buy a bottle of brandy or vodka, depending on what notion I took. I would drink that in my house before heading off to the pub. I might eat one meal in the day which was sure to be Kentucky Fried Chicken. I would usually eat in the evening when I was stoned out of my head. There were lots of days when I wouldn't have anything to eat at all. I hadn't a clue how much money I had blown, but that never really bothered me as I always had this vision that somehow I would stop drinking and turn my life around. I was really missing Karen now, so I called her and promised her I would give up my drinking if she came back. Karen said she was missing me as well, and, with that, she decided she would get the National Express coach down to London the next day.

While Karen was gone, I had been drinking with another hard case to whom I shall refer to as Jim. If Jim was in my house in the morning, then I would double up my order in the off licence and buy two bottles of spirits. I met Karen that Saturday evening at Victoria Coach Station and we were both delighted to be reunited. I had also a job lined up for Monday morning, so my intentions were good. On Sunday morning I asked Karen if she fancied going for one last drink with me. I now had my whole life figured out. Today I would have one good session and it would be my last. Tomorrow I would go to work and get my life back to normal. Karen said that when she got herself a job, we would get ourselves a nice little flat away from Acton, somewhere where we could both be on our own.

The Swakley Bar on Askew Road was as good a place as any for our last session. I figured it would have a live band playing until the first closing time at 3pm and I also knew I would meet a lot of friends there. We joined my old mate, Paul, and his lady friend whom Karen knew. Everything was going well until the barman called last orders and I now had an awful craving for more. After I bought a good round for my company, I then went back up to the bar and ordered ten more brandies for myself. The barman asked if I was I sure and I replied, 'Yes, keep them coming.' I picked up two at a time and placed them neatly on an empty table. The table was round and I had them sitting spaced out around the edge. I then said, 'If anyone would like to join me for a drink they should come quick as the drinks won't be sitting around for too long.' I sat at the table on my own and, one after the other, I swallowed the shorts down in quick succession. I then went back up to Karen and explained that, as it was going to be my last session, I wanted it to be a good one! I then asked Paul to come with me as I knew where we could find a party.

The girls said they would give it a miss and Karen said she would meet me later back at our house. On our way to the party we stopped at an off license in East Acton and bought a bottle of brandy and a bottle of vodka. We left the party again before 7pm and figured by the time we got back down to the Swakley it would be open again for business. As we were walking down, or probably staggering down, Acton High Street to get a taxi, I suggested we would go into the Kentucky Fried Chicken for a bite to eat. Paul put a cigarette into his mouth and asked the other customers for a light. There were two men and two girls sitting on high stools eating and one of them replied, 'Sorry mate, we don't smoke.' We were about to place our orders when one of the fellows takes a packet of cigarettes from his pocket and passes them around his friends. Well, Paul looks at me in disbelief, and at the same time the two men and two women are breaking their sides laughing at us. Paul and myself didn't think it was very funny and in the very next instant we punch the two men and knock them off their stools. That certainly put the laughing out of them! As they lay on the ground, we had two angry women screaming at us so we decided we would make a run for it.

We had just gone down the street a little bit when we were grabbed by two policemen and were told that we were under arrest. Karen and Paul's girlfriend arrived on the scene at the same time as we were being put into the back of the paddy wagon. Karen asked one of the policemen what the hell was going on and he snapped back and told her to mind her own business. Karen said it was her business as she lived with me! So that really put the cat among the pigeons because, when the policeman asked our address, she gave it to him. But I had already given them an old address.

Karen insisted on coming to the police station with us. They put me in a cell on my own and I soon fell asleep. Paul was locked up on his own as well, in the cell next to me. When they brought me out in the morning they handed me a charge sheet stating they were releasing me on police bail. My true and loyal friend Karen was still there waiting for me. As we both made our way back down Acton High Street that morning, we could see where someone had tipped over the rubbish bins. We later discovered it was my mate, Paul, who had been released sometime earlier.

It was too late now for me to report to my new job and, anyway, I was in no form for work. Karen and myself were both shivering with the cold so, after getting ourselves some breakfast, we decided we would go back to our house and sleep it off. I don't know how long we were in bed but we were awoken by a racket outside. It was my old mate Jim and he was raving drunk. He must have thought I didn't want to see him as he was talking aloud to himself saying, 'Now that the cunt has got his woman back he doesn't want to know me.' I opened up the door and said, 'Come on in you fucking head case.' He had one bottle of brandy for me and a bottle of vodka for himself. So much to my new start!

Once Jim sat down, he fell asleep. I brought my brandy upstairs and sat on the side of the bed. I was completely shattered and my mind was racing. Karen was lying, watching me and I knew she was worried and concerned and wondering where it would all end. I was supposed to be starting a new job, not drinking, and getting our lives back on track. But instead I now found myself with a bottle of brandy in my hand and out on police bail. I put the bottle to my head. I drank about a quarter of it and then turned to Karen and said, 'We need to get the fuck out of here.' When Karen asked where we would go, I said, 'We will go back to my home again, in Carrigart.' I was so relieved when Karen said she would come with me. When Jim finally woke up I had to break our news to him. Jim was gutted and said, 'Don't break the partnership.' He then suggested that the three of us should go to Manchester as he had friends there who would get us work and digs. I said I had my mind made up this time and if I got home safe and well I would never 'Fucking return again to this crazy city.'

All I had to do now was to get through the night, so I asked Karen to walk with me to the off licence. I was so weak and paranoid that Karen had to hold my hand like a baby as we crossed the busy street. Once again I bought two more bottles and Karen got enough groceries to make us all a good feed. I remember seeing the expression on Jim's face when we got back to the house with the carry out. 'Jesus, you're going to kill us,' he said. Karen made us all a good feed and we continued on drinking through most of the night. The next morning I ordered a taxi to take us to Heathrow, and suggested to Jim that he would be better off getting out of London. At this stage me and Jim were both in the horrors and still drunk. Jim agreed with me and said he would go to Dublin as he had a mate there that would give him a job. As the three of us jumped into the taxi Jim asked the driver to take him to his flat as he needed to collect his clothes and his tools. I told the taxi driver we didn't have time to be touring around London and take us straight to the airport. I then turned around to Jim, who was sitting in the back, and said to him, 'I'll buy you clothes and tools when we get to Dublin.'

At Heathrow Airport, Jim bought a disposable shaving set and went to the toilet to shave. But with the shakes he did more harm than good and his face was cut in several places. It was the first time I laughed that morning. Jim then declared that he had no ID with him and so couldn't come with us. I told him that I was both sad and glad to be leaving him! We both shook hands and wished each other the best. I made my way up to the ticket desk and bought Karen and myself two return tickets to Dublin. I swore to myself that morning if I got on the plane I would never again come back. I bought the return tickets, in case I was stopped and questioned about skipping my bail.

We did make it back to Carrigart once again. The contractor still hadn't started our renovations. I still couldn't get sober long enough to face reality and Karen and myself were just sort of living out of a suitcase. Karen left me again and went back home alone. I continued on drinking. One day my mate, Frank, was driving back to London and asked me if I wanted to go with him. On the spur of the moment, I said yes. So the two of us stopped off at a pub on our way. I was talking to Frank about Karen and said I would love to see her again. So he said we would call her and would stay in Newcastle for a night. Karen said it would be nice to see me, so after drinking quite a few hot whiskeys, Frank admitted he was in no form for driving and we would have to wait and go the following day. But I told him that if he didn't go right there and then, I wouldn't go at all. Looking back, you would think I was busy or something, and I never gave a second thought to Frank getting caught for drink driving. I had offered to drive myself but Frank said he would not sit in with me in a million years so the two of us set off and arrived at Karen's home many hours later.

We stayed one night in Karen's and, a few days later, Karen joined me in London to give it one more try. Sometime after that Karen's mother rang and asked could she come back home for a while and take care of the house, as she had to go away for some time with her job. Karen asked me to come with her so the two of us got the National Express from Victoria Coach Station up to Newcastle. I still had no income and after a week drinking in Newcastle, I decided once again that I was going home to try and sober up. I didn't have enough money on me for the fare so I rang my bank at home and told them to send £500 to Karen's address. The next morning I rang another mate called Rory, who was living and working in Leeds and explained my predicament. He told me to get the bus down to Leeds and he would meet me.

Meanwhile, Karen was at her wits end with me, and couldn't cope with my drinking or wild ways of living any longer. I told her I was going down to Leeds and we both wished each other the best as we parted company that day at Newcastle bus station. I had just about enough for the fare but knew I would be ok when I got to Leeds. That day I cried my eyes out on the bus. Rory met me at the station and gave me a good sub so, after another week in Leeds; I finally made it home again to Donegal. The contractors had just finished our renovations. I was lucky I had it done at that stage when I still had enough money to pay for it. I was sorry Karen wasn't around now to see it and enjoy it. But we had parted on good terms and with the understanding that it was finally over between us.

I hadn't told her I had ordered a cheque to her address but I had decided I was going to forget about it and let her keep it, as she had been so good and loyal to me. You can imagine my surprise when, two weeks later, I received a letter from Karen and my cheque enclosed. My bank had also made a big mistake and the cheque was for £5,000 instead of £500. In her letter, Karen said she was sorry for not posting it sooner. She didn't have the price of the stamp.

Chapter 31

St. Anthony Saves Me Again

With Karen now gone I seemed to be drinking more, if that was possible. I was also more inclined to get myself in trouble again. Myself and my brother Edmund entered a bar one evening that we were both apparently barred from. I didn't know what I had done to deserve a barring so I asked my brother Edmund what he had done. His reply was, 'Fuck all,' so once again, I felt like it was our reputation that had us barred and not our actions. In a situation where I feel I have been treated unfairly, I usually lose my temper. So, true to form, we started smashing up the bar. I later had to pay £600 for the damage caused during that incident.

Immediately after that incident, we entered another bar from which I was rightly barred. The barman there kept his cool and continued to serve us while he waited for the Gardaí to arrive. I'm sure he heard the commotion earlier and was probably expecting our visit. Only one Garda arrived and he asked me to leave, but I told him we would only come with him on the condition that he would drive us to another bar, where I knew we would both get served. He agreed and, as you can imagine, the landlord in the next bar was not impressed when he sees the patrol car pulling up at his door and Edmund and myself jumping out. The Garda refused our offer of joining us for a drink!

As long as I continued drinking I was living life on the edge and getting into crazy and dangerous situations. One other day, myself and a mate were on a pub crawl going from town to town. He was driving, so he asked me if I would be his co-pilot. Over the next few miles everything was going ok and I was keeping him informed of what route we were going. We were then driving down a road that was just straight for about two miles, but had a fairly sharp corner at the end of it, which veered left. We were now travelling at a fast speed and as we approached the corner my mate asked, 'Which way now co-pilot?' I was certain he knew the route himself, so I just thought I would call his bluff and replied, 'Sharp right.' Jesus, I couldn't believe it when he followed my instructions and in the next few seconds we both found ourselves crashing through a fence before ending up in an upside down car, half ways across somebody's field. The car was completely wrecked. We were both sore and bruised for a week or so but, thank God, we didn't receive any serious injuries. Needless to say that was our last rally together.

I remember being involved in two other car accidents which could have been fatal. In the first one, my mate fell asleep while driving. I was the front seat passenger and so I took hold of the steering wheel with my right hand trying to steer the car into safety. But by this stage my mate was slumped over with his foot on the throttle. We were both so drunk. We were now approaching a corner at a bridge, with a big drop into a river. I don't even think I knew what road we were on so, as you can imagine, we never managed to take that corner. Instead I found us in mid air before crashing into a tree which probably stopped us from ending up in the river. It was the passenger's side of the car that hit the tree. My mate soon woke up with the impact of the crash and asked me if I was ok. I was trapped in the car, which was now lying on its side. But I still had my crazy sense of humour and replied, 'No I'm dead, so just reverse her out!' My mate climbed out the front windscreen which was shattered. A neighbour had come on the scene and met my mate as he was climbing back up onto the road. He asked if there was anybody else in the car and my mate said, 'No, I'm on my own.' 'Well,' the neighbour remarked, 'it's a good job you were alone, as no passenger would have survived that crash.' It was only when the neighbour took a closer look at the car that he realised I was still in it. At this stage, my mate had got himself a lift to a nearby pub and was busy drowning his sorrows.

The second accident happened in completely different circumstances. I had just come out of a pub and noticed another mate getting into his car. I shouted at him and asked him to wait for me as I needed a lift. Well, either he didn't hear me, or maybe he just didn't want to give me a lift because he moved off as I approached. I just managed to reach the back door, got it open and scrambled in head first. The car was gathering speed and I was struggling to get my feet in and close the door. Jimmy, the driver, was out of his head on drink and the next thing I realised he was driving up a side road leading into a beach. I shouted at him to stop but he turned around and said, 'I'm going to drown you, you fat fucker!' So then I asked him, 'And what about yourself?' to which he replied, 'I'm going to drown myself as well.' I knew then he was completely gone in the head and, in my panic, I reached for the steering wheel. We were now fighting over the controls so the next thing I know we are careering up a large sand dune and the car flips over on its side. Jimmy manages to get out first and then shouts to me, 'Get out and give us a push to see if we can get her back on the road.' By the time I managed to climb out,

Jimmy had disappeared, so I set off walking for home. I heard later that Jimmy had gone for help to get his car out but could not remember where we had crashed it. It was later the following day when he found it again.

Chapter 32

Going to Glasgow

After the New Year in 1992, I once again decided I needed a change of scenery to make a new start for myself. It was only eight months since I received my compensation, although I could account for about £22,000 I had also managed to blow another £18,000. So I now had £50,000 left. I don't know what possessed me to go to Glasgow but that was where I landed, with my good intentions. After staying at a mate's house for a few nights I got myself a large room in a house. The landlord said he was registered and would accept social welfare, so I got myself registered with a doctor, was declared unfit for work and got signed on again at the local DHSS office. I also made a claim for my rent allowance. I now felt good having all that sorted. My next plan was to find myself a part-time job and ease up on my drinking and get my social life sorted out. The landlord said he kept a good house and would not tolerate any noise or messing about.

Well, true to form, once again I started on another serious bender. The rougher the bars, the more I seemed to blend in. After getting myself a date one night, I brought her home with me and just about managed to have sex with her. When I awoke the next morning, I was devastated when I realised she had gone. I'm not sure if it was because of my very poor performance or the fact that I had pissed the bed big time. One other night, I was in a nightclub and met a woman, who asked me which football team I supported. I told her that I didn't follow football. She then announced that her brothers would probably slit my throat if they caught us together. The following morning I woke up beside her in her house. The first thing I noticed was that the bedroom was covered in Rangers memorabilia. I turned around to her then and said, 'Hi honey. I think it's a bit early in the relationship yet for me to meet your family.' I then made a hasty exit.

One month later I was still in Glasgow and still on my bender. I was drinking brandy and remember losing my voice for a period. One day I woke up on the Glasgow to Donegal coach with no recollection of getting on it whatsoever. We were at Stranraer. I was alone on the coach as everybody else had gone on board. I checked my pockets for money and when I counted enough out, I got a ticket and got on the ship. I figured it would be my quickest way of getting a drink. I had no idea or plan at that moment where I was going to end up that day, but I needed a drink so bad that I would have sailed anywhere to get it. Once on board I was like a cat waiting on a mouse for the bar to open. When it finally opened, the ship was shaking and I was also shaking and almost collapsed when the barman said, 'I can't serve you, as you've had enough already.' I was too weak and in too bad a form to plead my case and was now in a bad predicament. Here I was on a ship that I didn't want to be on, with a barman who would not serve me. I was just about to turn and walk away when a lady, who had been talking with the barman, asked me what I was drinking. I told her that I'd love a brandy and port and was really grateful when I now found myself getting served.

The lady was smiling as she walked down to a table with her own drink and sat down alone. I was wondering to myself if she was travelling alone. Every time I looked down at her table she was smiling and just shaking her head at me. I was waiting for some man to join her. I figured he might have just been at the toilet or something like that. After four more drinks, I was now beginning to hit form again and, as my mysterious friend was still alone, I decided it was time to buy her a drink and join her at her table. When you meet someone for the first time you have so much to talk about. So after I thanked her for changing the barman's mind, I was then ready to interview her. I almost fell from my seat laughing when she told me what had happened. The previous night, I had met her in a club and she had told me she was going home to Donegal in the morning. I then obviously said that I needed a wee break myself and would come with her. Apparently, we continued on drinking until it was time to get the coach at the Gorbals. I must have been on auto pilot and once we sat down on the coach I fell into a comatose sleep. When I finally awoke at the boat my mind was a complete blank. I had no luggage or anything with me so I decided I would travel on to my home, in Carrigart, that day. My new friend and I arranged to meet at 2pm the following day, in Letterkenny, for a drink. We were supposed to meet outside Dillon's supermarket but I never made it. I was sorry afterwards, as I really enjoyed her company and she had a great sense of humour.

St. Anthony must have been with me at all times back then as I was really living life on the edge. Before I got the return bus back to Glasgow the following week, myself and another mate came crashing off his motorbike. We were travelling at a high speed when a dog crossed our path. Neither of us was wearing helmets and, although we both landed head first in a hedge, we were not badly injured. The bike did need a good bit of repair. Back in Glasgow again, I continued on my bender.

My landlord could not figure me out at all. He knew I wasn't working. One day he asked me how I could afford to keep on drinking. I told him that as long as he kept on getting his rent on time, he shouldn't be concerned about the money I was spending.

One night I met a woman in a bar and we were both having a good old session together. I asked her if she was working in the morning so she said, 'Why are you asking?' I told her I had the day off and that I'd like to meet with her again and we could both go for the cure. She then said to me, 'If you play your cards right tonight, you might wake up beside me in the morning.' Well, I must have played ok that night but I was not so lucky a few weeks later. I was on a pub crawl on my own. I was walking down a street at 3pm in the afternoon. I got approached by a nice lady. She didn't state her occupation but she said she would give me a blow-job for £10. After handing over the agreed price she set about her side of the bargain. Everything was going well until she suddenly jumped up and screamed, 'Run, the police are coming.' Now I was in a predicament. The police were coming instead of me and my lady friend had disappeared around a corner with my £10. After I got my trousers pulled up I ran after her shouting, 'Come back with my money, you whore.'

I ran into the first bar I came to. I was out of breath and was all flustered so, after ordering a drink, I went into the toilet for a piss. You can imagine my shock when I discovered I was still wearing a condom.

I went to my doctor again in Glasgow, for another cert. This time he asked me how my stomach was. I told him it was fine. But he warned me that with the amount of alcohol I was drinking, it was only a matter of time before my health was in serious trouble. I was surprised he knew what I was drinking, but he told me he had met me one night in a bar and after buying him a drink I ordered four more for myself. I didn't remember meeting him, but I was still in the habit of buying four drinks at a time for myself and I had to have them in four separate glasses. I was doing most of my drinking during the day in one particular bar. But I managed to get myself barred – myself and a mate got involved in a punch-up with some locals. I was also asked to leave another bar after the barman thought I was winding him up by ordering four drinks at once. He had already served me one round and probably was expecting three more people to join me. But he just stared at me with his mouth wide open when I just swallowed them one after the other.

I was capable of landing anywhere for a drink. One morning I got a flight into Dublin. After drinking there all day, and on my own, I returned that night to Glasgow on another flight. I was stopped by the airport police and, when I told them my only reason for going to Dublin was for a drink, they just looked at me and asked if I could not get one closer than that. I was now three months in Glasgow and hadn't sobered up in all that time.

I went home one weekend for my nephew's 18th birthday party. The party went well and everybody enjoyed it. A few days later, myself and two mates decided we would move to another part of the county for a drink. They were also two characters so we probably had to travel a bit to find a pub from which none of us were barred. After visiting a few different ones, Henry, who owned the car, asked me to drive as he was going for a sleep. I was all business and even stopped and lifted a hitchhiker. I asked him where he was going and when he said Dungloe I replied, 'You're in luck, as that's exactly where we are going.' Jesus, if he had said he was going to Hong Kong my answer would have been the same. Henry was snoring and Pat was singing his heart out. Meanwhile, I was laughing as we were driving down the road. The hitchhiker then announces that he wants to get out. But I see a pub ahead and I just swerve the car in towards it. I lost control and drove up onto the step and knocked down the down pipe from the wall in the process. I now have the doorway completely blocked. I must have been thinking that I was one of the lads from the Dukes of Hazzard because just then I climb out my door window. I fell into the pub door and, needless to say, I got refused a drink. So when I returned to the car, Pat was in the driver's seat and our hitchhiking passenger had disappeared.

The following morning I got the coach back to Glasgow. On our way into Larne I must have fallen asleep. When I awoke we were just about to go under a fly over bridge. I almost had a heart attack when I saw a large lorry driving across it. Jesus, I thought the bloody thing was flying in mid air! When I arrived in Glasgow I ended up in a late bar and when I arrived back at my lodgings my mate Paul was waiting for me. He told me he was going home for a few days. He asked me would I go down to the DHSS on Tuesday and sign on for him, as he would not make it back in time. I told him it would be no problem and said I would go down and wait with him until he got on his coach. We arrived down at the Gorbals early. I went into a newsagent shop and bought a large bottle of lucozade. As I was leaving, I then asked the gentleman behind the counter if he had anything stronger and I couldn't believe my luck when he reached down and produced a bottle of vodka. I then got two plastic cups and went out to my mate and said we would have a drink, while we were waiting. It was my first time drinking vodka and lucozade. By the time the coach arrived, we had almost finished the bottle so, as me and Paul are shaking hands, I suddenly thought to myself, 'What the fuck am I doing in Glasgow?' I had just arrived back the day before so here I am now, back on the coach for home once again.

I phoned my landlord some days later and told him I wouldn't be returning. I had left some clothes in my room but I wasn't too bothered and never returned for them. Back at home, my brother Edmund and myself decided we would make a home brew of beer. We bought a large plastic bin to brew it in and all the necessary ingredients. Of course, we couldn't be happy with following the proper instructions so we added extra yeast and sugar to make it extra strong. It tasted horrible but a few bottles of it would soon have you singing and that was what we both wanted. We didn't care about the taste. It was just the effect we wanted.

It was during this period that I wanted a wall built around our house. Edmund said he would manage the building and I agreed to labour to him. So a week later, after keeping him topped up with whiskey and home brew, the job was completed. Sometime after that, upon seeing the wall, Edmund asked who built it. He didn't actually remember building it himself. One other time Edmund and myself were helping our brother, Eunan, build a shed. Edmund had been a chef before and so he was in charge of the cooking, so when we went in to eat we found Edmund turning the chops on the pan with the cement trowel. Eunan refused to eat, so Edmund turned to me and said, 'Jesus, brother, that's now an extra chop we have to eat.'

Chapter 33

Continuous Benders in Dublin & Galway

Part of me was probably missing the buzz of being in a city. At home, my social life would mean having to get a taxi to Letterkenny, or some other town, for a nightclub. It was costly and hard work trying to get a taxi for the return journey home. It was then that I came up with the idea of going to Dublin for weekends. I would get the bus down, book myself into a B&B in the city, and hit the town. I used to enjoy the freedom and the choice of bars and clubs it gave me. It was during one of these trips that I met up with a girl from Dublin City. We saw each other for a while, before I fucked it up with my drinking again! One weekend I went down to Dublin and after I had booked myself into a B&B, I then met my friend and stayed at her house for three nights. When I finally went back to my B&B to collect my bag, the landlady met me and said, 'Jaysus, I thought you must have been bloody murdered.' So, after I failed to turn up for a few dates my friend gave me my P45.

I was also capable of landing in any part of Dublin, on any given weekend, but thank God I never did get into any bother there. It was also a good city if you wanted to drink 24 hours a day, which I always did when I was still awake. Looking back I must have pissed every bed, in every B&B, in and around Dublin City centre. After my mishap, I always felt very embarrassed. So I tried to make sure I didn't book the same place again. But on several occasions, I discovered a rubber mattress on my bed and figured I must have been there before, having left my trademark.

I had been thinking about going to America for some time. So, in order to travel to the States I had to get myself a passport and, with this in mind, I once again set off for Dublin. This time I brought my nephew, Seamus, with me as I figured, at the most, we would only have to stay for one night. After doing the necessary paperwork out at their offices in Ballsbridge, I was told I could collect my passport the following day. I then booked myself and Seamus into the Gate Hotel on Parnell Street. I did manage to collect my passport but it was eight days later before we left the Gate Hotel. I went on another serious bender and on the eighth morning I suggested to Seamus that we should go to London for a drink. Thank God, Seamus talked us out of it, so instead we got the bus back up to Donegal.

Another time I went down to Galway for a mate's wedding. I had been looking forward to it, as I knew I would meet up with a lot of old friends from London. The wedding was on a Friday so I got the bus down and arrived the night before. All the wedding guests were staying in the same hotel. The morning of the wedding, myself and three other guests were so drunk that we couldn't find the church in time and missed the actual ceremony. We did manage to reach the reception but I can't remember much about it. The following day, we left Galway in a four car convoy for the journey home to Donegal. We stopped off for a drink in a pub in Milltown and we ended up staying there overnight. The craic was mighty and the landlady gave us the use of a few bedrooms for us all to sleep it off. I woke up on Saturday morning at 7.30 a.m. and met a member of staff as I was coming down the stairs. She asked me if I wanted some breakfast but, of course, food was the last thing on my mind and, instead, I asked if there was any chance of a drink. She said it was no problem and so I started into the brandy and port. As the morning went on, the other guests appeared but none of them joined me at the bar. I suppose the ones who weren't driving didn't have the same problem as I had with the old bottle.

It was only when I was leaving that I realised I had left my bag behind me in the hotel in Galway. I had recently bought a nice leather jacket and didn't want to lose it, so instead of going home with my lift, I made my way back to Galway on my own. It was now late evening, so after getting reunited with my bag I then booked a room for the night. I remember being refused more drink that night at a disco in the hotel. I also remember sometime after that ordering drinks to my room. I think the night porter was pissed off with me as I had him running flat out for a while. The next morning I checked out and went to another bar in the town for a cure before getting my bus home. Well, it would have been a much wiser and cheaper option for me if I'd bought myself another set of clothes, because the following Thursday morning I was still in Galway. I had checked myself in and out of the hotel on five different occasions in the one week. I was in such bad form when I did get on the bus to Donegal, that when we stopped in Sligo, I priced the cost of a taxi home. But after consuming a large amount of alcohol in a bar, I decided I would get back on the bus for the remainder of my journey.

The following day I went into my local bar. The landlady advised me to seek professional help as "I was going to kill myself drinking." She did serve me two drinks, all the same, but said that was all she would give me. I was completely shattered and a nervous wreck so I then phoned my local doctor for an appointment. The doctor had no hesitation in referring me, for admission, to the psychiatric department at Letterkenny General Hospital. I then took this crazy notion that I might as well have one last good session before signing myself in. Being completely ignorant of my alcoholism, I had assumed that, once I presented myself to the hospital, the professionals would do the rest, and cure me immediately. A friend of mine was driving me to the hospital so I got him to stop off at a bar along the way. I was so fucked up with drink that night, I remember throwing my referral letter over the counter. The barman gave it back to my friend and that same night I finally arrived at the psychiatric unit and signed myself in.

When I awoke some hours later I was determined to leave again and had to be sedated to be kept from leaving. The following morning, I did sign myself out but against the doctor's wishes. I remember feeling so weak, it was a struggle trying to sign the form requesting my discharge. Looking back I probably only went into hospital out of sheer desperation, but I still hadn't addressed my problem.

Chapter 34

Stealing Two Garda Uniforms

I only managed to stay off the drink for three weeks after that. It seemed like ages at the time. One night, myself and a mate went to a dance in Letterkenny and for the first hour I only drank minerals. I just wasn't comfortable so I thought a few drinks would do no harm. I also figured that I would just wait until night-time to have my drink and not bother with it during the day. Well, that was wishful thinking. After the first four or five drinks that night I was feeling so good and so relaxed. I even questioned why I should torture and deprive myself of something that made me feel this way. Well, that's probably the feeling and experience a social drinker can expect at all times, but not me. I was an alcoholic and my craving for drink that night seemed greater and stronger than ever. Before we left the dance we bought two bottles of brandy. Once outside we got a taxi and, as were going down the road, I decided we should stop off at another mate's house and spend the night there. I also thought it would be handy for us in the morning, as we would be within walking distance to the pub. Then another brainwave hit me – I decided I would try and dodge paying the fare as I wanted to be sure that I had enough money for the following day.

I kept this plan to myself so I asked the driver to stop about six doors away from my mate's house. We were in a housing estate. I jumped out, carrying our two bottles and ran off in between two houses. I knew my mate's back door wouldn't be locked so I ran as hard as I could through back gardens to my intended address. I could also hear the commotion at the front of the houses between my mate and the taxi driver. I was laughing as I ran in the back door and upstairs to the room I knew my mate slept in. Well, I soon stopped laughing when I realised I had gone into the wrong house. There was a couple in bed and I must admit I really gave them both a fright. The lady was screaming and the man was going to box me, but when I apologised and explained what had happened they were ok about it. In fact, they also had a good sense of humour and the three of us then watched out the bedroom window as my mate and the driver continued to wrestle and argue over the fare. The driver now had my mate on the ground and was giving him a bit of a choking, while my mate was shouting for me to come back and pay the driver. When the driver finally realised that he wasn't going to get paid, he left. I then called my mate in then for a well deserved drink.

One other day another mate and myself were drinking in another town. It was a Sunday and there was only one bar where we got served. There was only one other customer in the bar and, not long after, my mate and him began to argue. The landlord told us he was closing up for a few hours as he had to cook the dinner. I thought it was a clever way of getting us out and avoiding a row. So I bought a bottle of whiskey and started walking down the street towards a friend's house. As I was walking past the Garda barracks, I noticed the door was open and, on the spur of the moment, I walked inside. I can't remember what was going through my mind at that particular moment but then I realised, 'I'm standing inside a Garda Station that I have no reason whatsoever to be in, with a bottle of whiskey in my hand'. I didn't see any Gardaí and it was all very quiet. It was then that I noticed the uniforms. Without another thought, I put on the Garda hat and coat. I walked back out again onto the street and could feel people looking at me. At this stage I was swigging out of my bottle. I was anxious now to get to my friend's house, before I got myself arrested so I decided I needed a taxi. I walked in the door of what I believed was the taxi driver's house and, once again, I discovered I had made the same mistake as before and was in the wrong house. I was met by a woman who could not believe what she was seeing. Here I was, dressed as a Garda, staggering and drinking from a bottle of whiskey. I then said to the woman, "I'm the new Sheriff in town and I believe you have poitín in your house." She was breaking her sides laughing at me and replied, 'Jesus, Guard, I have no poitín.' I then replied, 'Well, in that case you might as well have a drink of my whiskey.' By that stage both of us were in stitches.

I then went next door where the taxi driver lived. He looked at me from head to toe before agreeing to take me to my mate's house. As we were driving, I spotted Dan, who I had been drinking with earlier. He was driving a tractor, which he must have borrowed without the owner's permission. So I asked my taxi driver to stop immediately as I "wanted to get out and make an arrest." I jumped out, stood in front of the approaching tractor and signalled for Dan to stop. I should have known Dan better, as the next thing I know, he is increasing his speed and is driving straight for me. I was lucky to be just about sober enough to jump out of his way!

I walked the short distance then to my friend's house. Instead of taking the time to open the gate, I just climbed over the wooden fence. I went to the kitchen window and knocked on it. When my friend's wife sees me, she says to him, 'What the fuck did you do last night? There's a Garda out there!' We all had a good laugh when they realised it was me. Inside the house, I removed my uniform. It didn't take us long to finish the bottle of whiskey so once again I made my way back into town in search of another bottle. I left the uniform in the house. I met a fellow on the street whom I knew so, after giving him the money, he got me another bottle of whiskey from a pub I was barred from. I was now on my return journey back to my mate's house. Now, the first time I went into the barracks it was just a spur of the moment decision, but as I passed for the second time, I decided to chance my luck again. I went in, got another uniform, and came out wearing it.

I managed to make it up to my friend's house again, but I eventually landed back down the town creating mayhem. I had been in a few bars telling them to close, before trying to operate check points outside on the street. It was at this stage that I finally got arrested. When my friend heard I was locked up in the station he arrived with the first uniform and gave it back. He assumed it would help my case. The Garda at the desk asked him, 'Is there any more of our property in that house?', to which my friend replied, 'Why, are you missing much more?' I suppose at that stage nobody knew for certain what I got away with.

Chapter 35

Going to America

I had always wanted to see America. I had a mate living in Philadelphia so I booked a flight from Dublin to JFK Airport in New York. I also booked myself a seat on a coach that would take me to my mate's house in Philadelphia. I was only going for ten days, so I took two thousand dollars spending money with me. After arriving at my mate's house, we went for a drink and that same night we ended up at a disco bar. The following morning I awoke, but my mate had already gone to work. We had arranged to meet back at this house at 5pm. After I had a shower and got dressed I decided I would take a walk down the street and get myself something to eat. After that I went into a bar and got myself a bottle of beer. My mate had introduced me to Coors beer the night before, so as I was intending on taking it easy on the drink, I figured a few beers would do me no harm. I wanted to phone home so I went to use the payphone located inside the bar door. As I was trying to figure out how it worked, I was approached by a lady who asked if I needed help. I handed her the number I wanted to call and enough coins to keep me talking for a while. After my phone call, as I returned to the bar, I noticed my lady friend waving me over. She was along with another girlfriend, so I went over and thanked her for her help. I then bought them both a drink and joined their company.

Everything was going well and a few hours later everything was going even better, as Lisa's friend had now left so I knew I had scored. Then Lisa asked if I wanted to go back to her friend's house for a drink so, of course, I told her it sounded like a good idea so we bought a six pack at the bar. But I was thinking to myself that it wouldn't be enough so I bought two more for good measure. I was actually tempted to buy a bottle of brandy as well, but I was trying to keep it cool and go with the flow. In the midst of all the action, I had forgotten to phone my mate and let him know where I was. It was now after five and he probably would have been concerned and wondering where I was.

Lisa had her car parked outside the bar and didn't seem to be worried about drinking and driving. I was on a great high, lying back in the passenger seat as Lisa raced up the highway in her fancy little sports car. We seemed to be driving for ages before we finally arrived at her friend's house. After getting introduced I was delighted when her friend produced a bottle of whiskey saying, 'God that damn beer won't be strong enough for an Irishman.' And she was right! The craic was good, drinks were flowing. The next thing I knew, I was dancing with the two girls – slow dancing, Irish dancing and dirty dancing. Jesus, I was having a great time, but when I realised the time and thought about my mate I asked if I could make a phone call. When my mate answered the phone he asked where I was. Now by this stage the two girls are feeling and touching me all over so I reply, "I must have landed in heaven." I told him I hadn't a fucking clue, but assumed I was still in America as I hadn't got on a plane or crossed any water. I told him not to worry as I was in really nice company and I would see him the following evening, after he finished his work.

Later that night, Lisa and I went for a ride in her car. Speeding along the highway, she asked me if I had ever done coke. I told her I didn't, and she then said, 'Would you mind if I did some?' I told her I didn't mind at all. I hadn't a clue about drugs but I knew she was referring to cocaine. After travelling for a short distance we arrived at a house. I didn't know who lived there or what we were doing there, but after hooting the horn two men came out and came over to our car. Lisa told me to join her in the back seat as the two men got into the front seats. They handed a package to Lisa. We were back on the road once again, and when Lisa wasn't flat out snorting powder up her nose, she was flat out trying to get up on me. Even though I had a skinful of Coors beer and whiskey inside me, I was beginning to feel nervous and on edge. The man in the passenger seat kept turning around and asking Lisa where she picked me up. We then arrived at a bar and we all went inside for a drink. Once inside and surrounded by a large crowd of people I began to relax once more and started knocking back the brandies. Sometime later I asked one of the men what sort of a feeling the drugs would give me. His reply was, 'It will make you feel good, man.' So we headed back out to the car where he was going to sort me out with a fix. But Lisa then grabbed hold of my hand and said, 'Don't go. What you never had, you will never miss.' I took Lisa's advice there and then. I must say, thank God I did because with my addictive personality anything could have happened that night.

A few nights after that, I found myself walking down a street. I was alone and lost and felt frightened as it seemed to be a dangerous area. I knew the name of the street I was looking for and assumed it was within walking distance. But I was afraid to ask anyone for directions in case I asked the wrong character. They were all mostly male and black. I then went into a

Chinese restaurant and asked the waiter for directions. As he was giving them to me, he told me which streets were one way, but I then told him that I was walking. He looked at me and said, 'You don't want to be walking around here.' I decided to call a taxi from their phone box but was told I would have to wait for at least twenty minutes. I was now becoming really paranoid. I phoned my mate's house. His partner answered and I gave her the name of the street I was now stranded in. She said, 'Martin, you're in a bad neighbourhood." So she said they would come down and lift me whenever my mate arrived home. As I didn't know how long I would have to wait, I told her I'd chance it. I started off walking once more. I was flat out, praying to St. Anthony and trying to remember the best I could the directions I had been given earlier. I was walking for almost an hour before I eventually found the street I was looking for. St. Anthony had saved me once again.

Chapter 36

Still on My Binge in Philadelphia

My mother had a cousin who had emigrated to Philadelphia many years ago. I was anxious to meet him, so I phoned and told him where I was staying and we arranged to meet in a bar nearby. Sean was his name. We met at lunchtime and, after a few drinks, Sean said, 'There's not much craic in here, I know a good bar we should go to.' Sean was driving, so he told me to reach down underneath my seat. I did and I found two bottles of whiskey. I opened up one and, after taking a drink from it, I passed it over to Sean, who also took a good swig from it. We had about half the bottle drank as we arrived at the next bar. The craic was good and every person that came in joined our company. I remember counting twelve people at one stage. The whiskey seemed to be appearing from nowhere, so I was anxious to buy a round. I asked the barman to give a drink to everybody who had bought me one. He said to me, 'What the hell do you mean? The whole bar is after buying you a drink!'

Later on, Sean said that he would take me up to meet his family. We drove along, passing the bottle to each other. When we arrived outside his house his son came out to meet us, but before I had time to get out of the car, Sean drove off again without any warning or explanation. We continued on as before, passing the bottle to each other and I remember us driving through several red lights. We then arrived at another house and this time I did get inside. After a brief introduction to another family relative, I was asked to take a seat. The gentleman of the house then asked us to excuse him while he took his dog outside to go to the toilet. So, as they went out one door, Sean signalled for me to follow him, and we both then rushed out another door without even waiting to say goodbye.

That same night, I was supposed to visit neighbours of my parents who had also emigrated to Philadelphia. There were thirteen of them all present that night to meet me. But I never made it. I heard they had an SOS out searching for me. Sean and myself were too busy driving around Philly and drinking from our whiskey bottles to meet anyone. The following night, myself and my mate were drinking in some bar. We were both very drunk and were asked to leave. I had forgotten to tip the barman and when he confronted me about it one word led to another. The bar was huge and was located on a corner. So, myself and my mate came out one door, turned and walked up the adjoining street. We then turned into what we thought was another bar. It was only when the same bouncers approached us and asked to leave for the second time that we realised our mistake.

The family that I had missed dinner with finally caught up with me. Joan phoned my mate's house early one morning and asked, 'Where the hell were you the last night we had arranged to meet?' I said I was suffering from jet lag and fell asleep. Joan then quipped, 'Well, give me the name of the God damn airline you flew with and I guess I won't be flying with them.' I guess a lot of people had heard the story about me and Sean driving around and passing the whiskey bottle between us.

I was in a bar in Philadelphia at 7.30am the day I was due to return home. I don't remember leaving it and neither do I remember the bus journey down to New York. I do however, remember going into JFK Airport. I had four hours to wait until my flight was due to leave. When I was checking myself in, the lady at the desk advised me not to have any more drink. Needless to say, I ignored her and went straight to the bar. I did manage to get through security and while I was waiting to board, I got talking to a lady who was going to Ireland for the first time. Like me she was travelling alone. We were getting on so well that she got her seat number changed so we would be together. I told her I was on a career break, so we had planned to spend some time together in Dublin. I was so relieved when I made it on to the plane as I had been concerned I had too much to drink and was completely shattered. I was looking forward to getting some badly needed sleep and I had my lady friend's company to look forward to.

I was seated on the aisle seat. My friend was next to me and there was a man at the window seat. I was just talking to my friend, in my usual manner, and I can't remember if I used any swear words during our conversation. If I did, I wouldn't have meant anything by it, and definitely wouldn't have meant to offend anyone. I was surprised then, when the man told me to mind my language. I honestly didn't know what he was on about, so I told him to mind his business as I wasn't talking to him. Well, that really annoyed him so he said to me, 'You're nothing but a shame and a disgrace and I'm surprised you ever got through emigration in the first place.' Now I was getting really annoyed, so I told him it was a pity he was on his way to Ireland.

We were still on the runway at this stage and he had called for assistance to have me removed. He also said that I had threatened him, which I did not.

Jesus, I now wanted to clock him. My friend must have been sorry for changing her seat, as she was now caught in the middle of it all. The stewards approached me and told me I would have to get off the plane. By this stage, the man was really making a scene and was blowing it all out of proportion. As I reached for my hand luggage, I asked the stewards to ask my friend what really happened. I also put on my wee innocent face and went into details of how upset I was having to go home to my mother's funeral. I also added that I was an only child and I was very sorry if I had offended him.

After a brief talk with my friend, the stewards took me down to a seat at the back of the plane. Once I got seated and had nobody to talk to, I soon fell into a deep sleep. I'm not sure how far into our flight we were when I woke up again. I was so thirsty and dry that my mouth felt like the inside of an old slipper. I could hardly speak so I signalled to the air hostess. When she came over, I asked her for a drink. She said that if I was lucky I might get a glass of water. After pleading my case, I managed to get a few cans of lager that kept me going until we finally touched down at Shannon. We didn't have much time to spare before our short flight to Dublin but I was so relieved to be back on Irish soil again that I didn't care if I missed it. I was enjoying a drink at the bar and I could hear my name being called to board. I was undecided on what to do and didn't even care about being separated from my luggage.

I decided to get back on and, once again, I boarded the plane. I was now met by a different air hostess, who was obviously unaware of our earlier incident. She asked me for my boarding card so when I showed it she showed me to my seat. As it was the same boarding card, I now found myself heading back to the seat I had been removed from. When my old friend saw me approaching he put his hands up in the air and screamed, 'Keep him away from me, he is an animal!' The air hostess rushed down and directed me into another seat. I was just about seated when a gentleman came down and said, 'You're sitting in my seat!' Jesus, it was just like playing musical chairs, so once again I had to get up. I just stood for the remainder of the short flight into Dublin. I had a good laugh talking to the air hostesses, as they were asking me what really happened between myself and the gentleman in New York. I told them that I didn't mean to offend anyone and that I was surprised when he confronted me in the first place. I also added that I felt a bit hard done by when I was moved from seat to seat. Well, they promptly replied, that if they had detected the amount of alcohol I had consumed, I would have been refused permission to board in the first place.

Chapter 37

Jersey

Another time when I was on a bender, I landed myself in Jersey. After booking into a B&B, I went into a nearby pub. That night I ended up at a disco. After it was over, I joined a large queue of people at a taxi rank. I was talking to another couple, when a gentleman standing in front started imitating and making fun of my broad country accent. Everybody was now laughing, except me of course. I then asked the couple I had been having the conversation with if there was much trouble on the island. They said they had been living there for two years and had seen no trouble at all. At this stage, I had made my mind up that I was going to box the man who was taking the piss out of me. It was my first night on the island and even though I was alone and didn't know who, or what I was dealing with, I still lashed out and hit him without warning. He fell back into the crowd, so I just walked off and decided I would make my own way back to my B&B.

I was walking around in circles for about two hours before I eventually found it. Jersey was pretty much the same as everywhere else I had been. I just continued on drinking for the duration of my stay there. One morning, I asked my landlady where I could get an early drink. She gave me the keys of the residents' bar. She told me that she didn't have time to serve me but I could help myself and just take a note of what I drank. We had that same arrangement several mornings after that.

The morning I was leaving I went into the bar beside my B&B for a drink. I had planned on getting a taxi from there to the airport. I can't remember how long I had been there when the phone rang. The barman answered it and then asked me my name. I couldn't believe it when he then said, 'There's somebody coming now to take you to the airport.' I was surprised and delighted when my landlady suddenly walked in. She said, 'I had a feeling I would find you here.' Only she arrived for me that day, I would have certainly missed my flight. In fact, I might still be in Jersey on a bender!

Chapter 38

The Death of My Father and Three Mates

That same year, 1992, a mate of mine died. It was a big shock to me. I suppose it started me thinking about my own life. My father said to me on several occasions that he would love to see me settle down. He was now getting on in years and I knew he wouldn't always be around. He was a smart man and he probably knew his time left on this earth was short. There probably would have been signs or whatever of his ailing health, but I was just too fucked up with drink to notice.

On the 20th March 1993, my father took a turn for the worse. He was up at my sister's house. My mother, two sisters and two brothers were with him. I was drinking in a bar about a 45-minute drive away. So they sent my mate to lift me. When he arrived at the bar, the Gardaí were already there looking for me, for a different reason. A fight had started and the barman wanted us removed. We left the bar and nobody got arrested. When I got back to my sister's house, my father had already passed away. It is one regret I will have for the rest of my life. I was not there for him when he needed me most.

Over the next four months, two more very close mates also died and I hadn't sobered in all that time. I was in the horrors and was convinced that I was going to die myself, if I didn't get help and change my ways. One day, I was alone in my house. It was about six months after my father had died. He appeared to me in our hallway. I was just staring at him and I was speechless. It was a strange, but comforting, experience. I remember thinking at that moment, 'This can't be for real, it must be my imagination.' I also remember reaching out and trying to touch Daddy. Although I know that day I was suffering from the horrors, I'm convinced my Daddy did come back to me, to let me know that he was watching over me and to help me get myself sorted. Later that evening, my mother asked me if I would like to talk with someone. I said I would like to talk to our parish priest.

I was in a bedroom, but was so bad with my nerves and paranoia that I climbed out the window. Once on the roadway, I managed to stop a car and got a lift to a pub. As we were driving down the road, we met the parish priest who was on his way to see me. Sitting at the bar that day, I was so bad with the shakes that I remember taking my drink into the toilet and using both my hands to raise it to my mouth. About an hour later I rang my mother. She told me she was shamed that she had brought the priest into the room only to discover that I had gone out the window. I asked her if he was still there and that I wanted to talk to him. So she put him on the phone. I told him where I was and he came down to the pub to see me. When he came in we shook hands and I said, "Father, I'm sorry for not waiting on you. I went out the window as I didn't want my mother to know I was gone." He said, "Martin, I understand. You needed a cure."

We then had a good talk about anything and everything and as he got up to leave, he shook my hand again and said, 'Maybe after this you will ease up on it?' I continued on drinking for one week after that. During that week, I remember being at home and going through the horrors and imagining the ceilings were bursting with water pouring down and drowning me. I raced into the next room to escape but only to experience the exact same thing again. I then called the doctor. I was sitting on the bed, in the same room that I had done the runner on the priest. I was drenched in my own sweat. The doctor came in and was holding a jar of tablets in his hand. He then asked my brother to bring us in a glass of water. Jesus, I was so far gone I thought the doctor wanted the glass of water for himself, so I then shouted out to my brother, 'You better bring me in a glass as well.' My brother often told that craic afterwards.

I'm not sure how many days my tablets were supposed to last, or how strong they were, but I do know that the following morning I was still awake and hadn't slept a wink. I had finished the full course of tablets during the night. started drinking again that morning at 7.30am. Later I arrived in a bar and got refused a drink. I just flipped and began smashing up the place. I'm not sure how much damage I had caused before I left, but I then went to the bar next door. Funny enough, I did get served there. A short time later, the landlord said that the Gardaí had arrived next door. 'Well,' I replied, 'don't worry I won't have them calling in here looking for me.'

I then walked out and straight back into the bar that I had just smashed up. The landlord and the Gardaí were now assessing the damage, so I just shouted, 'Ok boys, let's get the fuck out of here.' I walked out and jumped into the patrol car before the Gardaí came out. Mind you, it's probably a good job that the keys weren't left in the ignition! For some silly reason, I thought that the Gardaí would just leave me home but when they went in the opposition direction I asked, 'Where the fuck are we going now?' The Garda in the passenger seat turned to me and said, 'You're in serious trouble now, Martin and you will be in Mountjoy Prison tonight.'

They took me to the station, charged me, and later that same day my case was heard at a special sitting of Castlefin District Court. I had a Garda sitting on each side of me and the drink was dying inside me. I could feel myself going into the horrors once again. One of the Gardaí then asked me if I had much money, as I'd need to employ a good solicitor. I told him I needed all my money for drink and I wanted legal aid.

I did get legal aid that day. My case was called and in fairness to the Gardaí and the landlord, they didn't go against me. They were probably thinking that I had enough of a struggle ahead with my severe addiction to alcohol. I was released on my own bail. My case was adjourned for one month, to give me time to seek professional help and address my problem.

Chapter 39

Signing Myself into St. Conal's Hospital – For the Second Time

Two days after that I was so bad with the horrors, I was convinced I was going to die. I was still drinking but, as the saying goes, I was past the stage where a few drinks would make you feel any better. I was well and truly beat. I knew I had to go into the psychiatric unit of my local hospital again for professional help. This time I was determined to see it through. I rang my good friend the Parish Priest and told him my plan. I asked him if he'd say a prayer for me. But he said something to me that day I will never forget. He said "Martin, if you go up there now and sign yourself in, you will never look back." It was 29th September, 1993. I had only £4,000 left out of the £90,000 compensation I had received on my birthday on 3rd May 1990. Although I could account for about £20,000, I had managed to blow £66,000 inside three and a half years.

I had no qualifications, very little education, no car or even a drivers licence, no job and was now severely in the horrors of drink. There was also a good possibility that I would receive a jail sentence at the end of it all. Things were not looking very good that day but after hearing the reassuring and positive words from my Parish Priest I rang a friend and asked him to drive me up to the hospital. As I waited for my lift, I went for a short walk up the field behind our house. I remember thinking and saying to myself that day, "If I do get myself out of this mess, it will be a long time before it happens again." I also cried my eyes out on that lonely walk.

I did go and sign myself in that evening and I remember asking if could go into a ward on my own. I could hear all these voices going through my head and I was afraid to go to sleep, as I was certain I was going to be attacked by the other patients. I did punch another patient, who I imagined was going to attack me on my first night there. I apologised to him some days later when I started to recover.

He was very understanding of my situation and had only been coming to say hello and to ask me if I needed anything. It was such a shame.

During my stay there, I was introduced to an alcohol addiction counsellor. When I got out, I started attending his group therapy course on a daily basis. It was a six week course. It was a 30-minute drive each way from my home. I was lucky enough to get a lift each day with a neighbour, who was working close by. It also had the advantage of me being at home each night in my own safe and familiar surroundings.

I would say in the beginning my counsellor had his doubts about my intentions. He might have been thinking that I was only using the course to save me from the courts. Being totally honest about it, I was hoping it would save me from going to prison, but it was not my main reason for being there. I had finally admitted to myself that I was an alcoholic and I was determined to avail of any help or guidance that would help to keep me sober and allow me build a better life for myself. After I got over my first week, I used to look forward to attending. I built up a good friendship with the other people from my group, who were all in similar situations as my own, or somewhat worse. It was not all doom and gloom and there were some funny incidents.

I remember one day in our group, my counsellor asked me to throw my chair through the window. I refused. She then asked, 'Why not? Sure that's what you did in the public house.' 'Well,' I replied, 'that was different, because I was drunk that day.' She then said, 'So it was ok for you to do it because you were drunk. How do you know you won't be drunk tonight?' So I made a deal with her. I said, 'I'll tell you what we will do. Give me a bottle of whiskey now and the choice of drinking it or throwing the chair.' She replied, 'And what will you do?' I answered, 'I'll fire the fucking chair!' She then asked, 'And what will we do with the bottle?' I replied, 'As we are all alcoholics in this room, we might as well give the bottle to whoever fixes the window.'

One other morning, our counsellor wrote on his blackboard: 'I can't means I won't.' He went on to explain that if he asked me to go to the shop and if I said I can't, it was just the same as saying I won't. He continued, 'You could if you wanted to.' Well, I argued that it was not always the same. I added, 'If you were to give me a difficult sum to do now, I wouldn't be able to do it, but if I could, I would but I can't.' We all had a laugh at that.

My court case came up again. This time, my counsellor went up with me and spoke very well on my behalf. My case was then put back to be heard in three months time. After my six week course was completed, I then signed a contract undertaking to attend 'After Care' for a period of one year. It was only one day per week. It felt strange but it also felt great to be sober. At first, I found myself just walking into bars without realising. Sometimes, I would just walk out again and other times I would stay and have a mineral. My counsellors advised me to keep out of the bars for a while, as it was still a bit too soon into my sobriety.

Chapter 40

Meeting Liz

After I got my provisional licence, I bought myself a car. It was a 1982 Ford Fiesta. Although it didn't look very flash, it was in good working order. It cost me £400. My only income at this time was unemployment benefit and I had spent the remainder of my compensation. My court case had also come up and I was handed down a three months suspended sentence. It was suspended on the condition that I completed 150 hours community work at our local football club. I felt very relieved that my case was finished and I was looking forward to getting my community work over and done with. I must add, that the gentleman who was supervising us treated us with great respect and made our task much easier.

I was now also beginning to enjoy my social life again. I was able to travel to nightclubs that would have been out of bounds before as I was now driving. It gave me a lot of freedom. I would like to add that on St. Patrick's Day that same year, I got an awful urge to drink. Myself and my nephew were at the parades in Buncrana. Thank God, he talked me out of it, as I'd only been sober for less than six months. I also had taken an interest in myself and my appearance around this time. I had started exercising, mainly walking, and had managed to lose three stone in weight. I was also very lucky that I didn't need a drink to boost my confidence or to help me make conversation with the opposite sex. I found it relatively easy to approach a woman in a nightclub and ask her for a dance or a date.

One Saturday night, I drove 30 miles to a venue that had a live band playing. I was walking to the toilet when a girl stopped me and asked if I would take her friend out for a dance. She pointed out her friend to me and so I was very happy to oblige. So, full of confidence, I approached her friend and asked her for a dance. But she refused. When I turned to walk away she grabbed my hand and said, 'Ok maybe I will.' Her name was Liz. Later that night Liz asked me where I was and what I was doing on 29th September. I told her, very honestly, that it was the day I went into St. Conal's hospital to get dried out. So I asked Liz the relevance of the date. 'That's my birthday,' she said. Jesus, I thought, that was a huge coincidence. That first night Liz also told her friend, 'I've just met the man I'm going to marry.'

Chapter 41

Liz & St. Anthony

Seven years later, I was still sober and got married to Liz. It was the year 2000. I was 37 years old and had made a full recovery from my accident. A lot of changes had also taken place in my personal life. My nephew, Joseph, died in May 1998. Later that same year, in October, my mother also died. My brother Edmund died seven years later in September 2005. When you lose the people you love, it can change your outlook on life. Small trivial things that played on your mind, suddenly didn't seem that important anymore. Although I was sober, I could still become very restless within myself. I had started working in Seagate, in Derry, but just walked out one evening and never returned. Liz and myself had also bought a house in Strabane, Co Tyrone, but again, I became unsettled and one day I walked out and went back home alone to Carrigart. We later sold our house in Strabane. It doesn't matter how many houses or what property you own because, at the end of the day, the most important thing you can have in your life is a happy home. That could be a caravan, a mobile home or maybe just an old run down shack. We all like a bit of comfort, but money can't buy health or happiness. If I hadn't met Liz, I don't think I'd be here today.

Liz never drank and that had a huge bearing on my sobriety. We generally avoided the local pub scene in the early years and that prevented me from getting myself into awkward situations. However, one year into our married life, I took the crazy decision to drink once again. It wasn't just a spur of the moment decision, I had it planned for some time and had booked myself a weekend trip to London. Despite having a great life, the love and support of a great woman, a permanent job at Letterkenny General Hospital and a full driving licence (I finally passed my test), I broke out on the drink once again. I arrived in London as planned, and went into the Windmill pub in Acton and ordered myself a pint. It was a strange experience. Every time I finished a drink, I went to the toilets to see if I was still sober and ok. After five or six drinks I wasn't worried how I was, so I started phoning old drinking buddies and former housemates. That first night went according to plan, but once I awoke the following morning I was back to square one again. I hadn't time to shit or shower and couldn't get out the door quick enough for more drink. The following day, I was going home to Liz and I didn't want her to know I had been drinking. Although my form was bad that day I suffered and made it home.

I thought my plan had gone ok, so about a year later I tried it again. This time I wasn't so successful and ended up going off on a serious bender, on my own. It lasted two weeks and during that time I had travelled to Newcastle and also down to Liverpool. One morning, in Liverpool, I decided I would go to mass, as I was trying to get sobered up for my journey home. I ordered a taxi, and on our way to the chapel the driver asked me the price of drink at home. He then offered to sell me a bottle of vodka at £5. Jesus, I had planned on going to mass to pray to get sober but instead I ended up buying the bottle of vodka. After a few good swigs from the bottle, I soon forgot about mass, and home was then the last place I wanted to be. A few days later, I did manage to make it home but I continued on my drinking spree and ended up getting another flight back into Newcastle. I had changed as far as getting into trouble was concerned, but my craving for alcohol was just as strong as it had been all those years earlier. I was also still capable of landing in any part of the planet, on the spur of the moment.

After getting off that bender, I had a few more relapses. One other time, I started drinking in Glasgow. I went on a bender and went on tour. I also ended up in Leeds for two days and then decided to go to Newcastle for a night. I had switched my mobile phone off, as there was an SOS out for me back at home. I didn't bother buying a ticket for my train journey and, as the train pulled out of Leeds railway station, I realised I had lost my wallet which contained my passport, bank card and Visa card. Whatever money I had was in my pocket. When the Inspector on the train asked for my ticket I told him I lost it with my wallet. So, when I arrived in Newcastle, I rang the Police in Leeds to report my big loss. I could hardly believe my luck when they told me that my wallet had been found on the platform in Leeds railway station, with all my contents still inside. Once again, my prayer to St. Anthony had been answered. The policeman told me I had to call into the lost property office in Leeds Police Station to collect my wallet. I was now too busy drinking in Newcastle and decided I would try and get a flight home without my passport. So I had the idea to buy a weekly train ticket and attach a passport sized photograph to it. At Newcastle Airport, I showed my ID and it was accepted. When I finally got home and sobered up, I rang Leeds Police Station once again and asked them if they would they post my wallet home. A few days later, my prized wallet arrived through my letterbox.

Another time, I went on a bender which took me to Dublin, Monaghan, Cavan and Longford. I remember one other day being at work and feeling restless again. I figured I just needed to get away on my own. I booked an appointment with my doctor and hoped to get a cert declaring me unfit for work. I would then be able to claim disability allowance so I wouldn't be losing out financially. When I went to see my doctor, I was disappointed to discover that he was off on leave. His replacement didn't know my form, so I thought to myself that I won't have much bother bluffing her. Some of my drinking buddies in London had told me, if you ever had to bluff a doctor or the medical board, use either your nerves or your back as your complaint, as both are impossible to prove you wrong on. After I complained about my severe backache, my doctor asked how much pain I was in. I said, 'Doctor, you know nothing about it. I haven't slept for three nights.' After a struggle to get me up onto her examining couch, she then returned with a large needle. Jesus, I didn't want a needle stuck in my arse, but I had no option other than to play along. After getting my unwanted injection the doctor then declared me unfit for work for three days. But I wasn't happy. I said to her, 'Jesus, Doc, if you don't give me a cert for at least a week I won't receive any money from the social.' I got my cert for the week and hopped down from the couch. She told me it would take about 20 minutes for the injection to work, but I said, 'Doc., I'm feeling much better already.' Well, she laughed at that and wished me well. I had the cert but I had to suffer a sore arse for a few days for good measure.

I booked myself a flight to Newcastle against Liz's wishes. I promised her I wouldn't drink but I knew deep down I was going to, once I got loose and out of town. I don't think anybody sets out to overdose on the drink and put themselves through the horrors, but that's exactly what I did. I went off on an awful bender in Newcastle, for three days and nights and missed my return flight home. The following day, I booked another flight and missed that as well. The next morning, I ordered a taxi to take me to the airport. I was after drinking a bottle of whiskey to try to settle my nerves for my journey ahead. At Newcastle Airport, there was only one flight available for later that day. It was flying into Belfast City Airport. I booked it and although Liz said she would collect me, I knew I was in for a grilling. Liz did meet me in Belfast and said she would give me one last chance. I went through hell again for the next three to four days and nights. I just stayed in my room and Liz got some medication from my Doctor to ease my paranoia and help me from going into the horrors. Although you couldn't cope without professional help or medication, there is no magic wand or quick fix cure for alcoholism. But there is one sure thing, you will go to hell and back on the road to recovery. It's now two years since my last drink. I do think about alcohol every day, but I also think about how lucky I am to be sober once again.

Looking back on my life now, I think I'm a better person because of my experience. If you do go through a rough spell in your life, you learn to really appreciate things when life is good. The only regret I have is all the worry I caused my parents, and also the fact that I wasn't sober for my father when he needed me most. When some people tell me that they wished they were young again, I tell them that I certainly wouldn't want to be young again. I pity the young generation today, who are faced with not only drink, but also drugs. I never attended AA so I owe my sobriety today to Liz, whose love and support and understanding helped me with my struggle. I also give huge praise and devotion to St. Anthony.

I can't remember exactly what age I was when I started praying to my favourite saint, but from my early years, I remember saying his Novena of The Nine Tuesdays. St. Anthony is known throughout the world as the Saint of Miracles and he has certainly answered my prayers many times. Myself and Liz had the privilege of visiting his tomb in Padua, Italy, on four separate occasions. One of our visits was on his Feast Day. St. Anthony died on Friday 13th June, 1231. On his Feast Day this year, which is also Friday 13th, it will be 777 years since St. Anthony's death. One of the many favours I asked St. Anthony was for his help to remain sober. I still get restless from time to time and do go off on my own, but if I can keep away from the evil of alcohol, I don't have any other fear of life. It was along these same thoughts that gave me the title for this book, Sober, I am not Afraid.